AMERICAN
NOTES

The Western Frontier Library

Rudyard Kipling after he won the Nobel Prize for Literature in 1907.
Courtesy of the Library of Congress.

AMERICAN NOTES
—
RUDYARD KIPLING'S WEST

by
Rudyard Kipling

Edited
and with an Introduction by
Arrell Morgan Gibson

UNIVERSITY OF OKLAHOMA PRESS : NORMAN

Library of Congress Cataloging in Publication Data

Kipling, Rudyard, 1865-1936
    American notes.

(Western frontier library; 54)
    Includes bibliographical references and index.
    1. United States—Description and travel—1865-1900. 2. United
States—Social life and customs—1865-1918. 3. Kipling, Rudyard,
1865-1936—Journeys—United States. I. Gibson, Arrell Morgan.
II. Title. III. Series.
E168.K56 1981   917.3'0486   81-40289
                                            AACR2

New edition © copyright 1981
by the University of Oklahoma Press, Norman,
Publishing Division of the University of Oklahoma.
Manufactured in the U.S.A.
First printing.

CONTENTS

ILLUSTRATIONS

MAP

Caricature of Rudyard Kipling.
Reproduced from *American Notes* (New York: Books, Inc., 1910).

EDITOR'S INTRODUCTION

"America watching" was a popular nineteenth-century pastime. Many visitors from abroad published their impressions of American society. The best-known of this genre are Frances Trollope's *Domestic Manners of the Americans* (1832), two volumes; Alexis de Tocqueville's *Democracy in America* (1835), two volumes; Charles Dickens's *American Notes* (1842), two volumes; and James Bryce's *The American Commonwealth* (1888), two volumes. A fifth report on American society was popular and heatedly controversial at the time of its publication, but rather quickly was overshadowed by the subsequent distinguished literary output of its author: Rudyard Kipling's *American Notes.*

Kipling's *American Notes* for several reasons must be resuscitated and restored to its proper place among the nineteenth-century studies of American society written from the European viewpoint. First, that an author so completely identified "with India landscapes, cockney soldiers," *The Jungle Book,* and *Captains Courageous* would produce a book about Western America must come as a surprise and generate a sense of discovery.[1] Second, it differs from the other books of its kind by that group of distinguished authors in that it is the most westerly of these writings on the United States: most of its content focuses on the territory between Omaha and San Francisco. Third, as a travel narrative, its direction runs counter to the classical east-to-west concourse of empire: Kipling's itinerary was from West to East, which provides a novel viewpoint for geographic and social interpretation. Fourth, Kipling was the most environmentally oriented of these writers. Fifth, Kipling interjected polemic for con-

[1]"Elusive Storyteller," *Saturday Review* (September 6, 1975), p. 28.

vii

servation to be applied to the plundered western wilderness. Sixth, his arrival in the West was timely: the old order was passing, and a new one aborning; as a perceptive young journalist, he sensed this and reported it. Seventh, unlike the authors of the other works, which are consistently serious presentations, Kipling ran a skein of humor, if sardonic, through his narrative; he made copious use of hyperbole and was the most vituperative in his comments about American society. Finally, Kipling's mission to the United States had far more complex personal motivations than was the case for the other writers listed above.

Kipling was born in Bombay, India, on December 30, 1865, of British parents in the Indian service. When he was six, his parents sent him to England for his education. Kipling returned to India as a young man and worked as a newspaperman for the *Allahabad Pioneer.* Very shortly he became known locally as an aggressive journalist and the popular author of short stories and articles that lampooned high officials in the Indian congress and the imperial government of India. This made him an embarrassment for the *Pioneer* editor, who decided it best to remove Kipling from the scene by sending him to the United States to write feature articles on American society for the *Pioneer.* The young writer took his exile gracefully, but the cause of his banishment from India indicated a daring and irrepressible spiritedness, which would flavor his *American Notes* and other writings.[2]

Kipling sailed from Calcutta on the *Madura* in early March, 1889, stopping briefly at Rangoon, Penang, Singapore, Hong Kong, and Canton before arriving in Japan, where he spent nearly a month. In a Nagasaki bookstore Kipling found books containing his writings, pirated (he called them "burglaries") by an American firm, the Seaside Publishing Company. In a rage the young author placed a curse on Seaside and the people of the United States:

Because you steal the property of a man's head, which is more his peculiar property than his pipe, his horse or his wife, and

[2]See Angus Wilson, *The Strange Ride of Rudyard Kipling: His Life and Works* (New York, 1978), for a recent biography.

because you glory in your theft and have the indecency to praise or criticize the author from whom you steal, and because your ignorance . . . leads you to trifle with his spelling. [Inasmuch as] you print the stolen property aforesaid very vilely and uncleanly, you shall be cursed with this curse from Alaska to Florida and back again. Your women shall scream like peacocks when they talk, and your men neigh like horses when they laugh. You shall be governed by the Irishman and the German, the vendor of drinks and the keeper of vile dens, that your streets may be filthy in your midst and your sewage arrangements filthier. . . . You shall prostitute and pervert the English language, till an Englishman has neither power nor desire to understand anymore. You shall be cursed State by State, Territory by Territory, with a provincialism beyond the provincialism of an English country town. . . . Your hearts shall be so blinded that you shall consider each one of the curses foregoing a blessing to you as it comes about, and finally I myself will curse you more elaborately later on.[3]

And Kipling kept that promise.

American publishers were notorious for pirating foreign works, especially English writings, and printing them on cheap stock with paper covers. The pirated works sold for a dime or so in stores and railway stations. People read them while traveling and in other idle moments, then cast them aside. Kipling despised literary pirates, and he placed the blame for their existence on the American people because it was in their power to obtain laws which would curb these larcenies. Later he amplified his position, saying "This may sound bloodthirsty; but remember, I had a grievance upon me—the grievance of the pirated English books." The curse for theft of his literary properties is cast in the context of his sardonic humor: "Oliver Wendell Holmes says that the Yankee school-marm, the cider, and the salt codfish of the Eastern States are responsible for what he calls the nasal accent. I know better. They stole books from across the water without paying for 'em, and the snort of delight was fixed in

[3]Luther S. Livingston, "From Sea to Sea," *The Bookman* 9 (July, 1899): 431.

their nostrils forever by a just Providence. That is why they talk a foreign tongue today." Thus he claimed a retributive deity had righted justice by confounding the speech of Americans.[4]

Kipling sailed from Yokohama aboard the *City of Peking* and arrived in San Francisco Bay on May 28, 1889. His store of anti-American bias, already substantial because of the instinctive British contempt for "colonial upstarts," and his resentment at the United States for harboring and abetting literary pirates were fed by a disappointment soon after he disembarked. Kipling offered some articles to the San Francisco *Examiner* editor, who agreed to buy them if Kipling would smooth out "one or two raw spots." But Kipling was adamant: "not a line, word, or even a comma" was to be changed, and, when his writings were re-

[4]George H. McKnight, "Kipling's View of Americans," *The Bookman* 7 (April, 1898): 132. The first American copyright law, passed in 1790, allowed an author to copyright his work for fourteen years with one renewal for fourteen years. Foreign writers received no copyright protection in the United States, and American publishers were notorious for pirating foreign works for which the authors received no royalties. Most of the major countries of the world, unlike the United States, adhered to the Bern Convention of 1887, which provided that material copyrighted in a signatory country was automatically copyrighted in all the signatory countries. Congress finally adopted a more protective copyright law in 1891, which permitted copyright of works by foreign authors but required that foreign works in English be manufactured (printed and bound) in the United States. In 1909 that law was amended to increase copyright protection to twenty-eight years with one renewal for an additional twenty-eight years. At Geneva in 1954 most of the leading nations, including the United States, signed the Universal Copyright Convention, which went into effect September 16, 1955. Its purpose was primarily to bring the United States into a general system of international copyright. Congress accordingly modified the federal copyright statutes to conform to the commitment, including elimination of the requirement that works in the English language by foreign authors must be manufactured in the United States to receive federal copyright protection. In 1976, Congress again amended the federal copyright statutes to continue current copyright duration for twenty-eight years from the date when originally secured and to increase the renewal extension to forty-seven years if application for renewal and extension is made one year before the original expiration date. Works created on or after January 1, 1978, are copyrighted for the life of the author plus fifty years after his death.

jected, Kipling exploded that the editor had "declined my stories! The bally ass said they weren't up to the standard of the *Examiner*." This compounded his anti-American bias.[5]

From San Francisco, Kipling traveled by rail north across Oregon and Washington to Vancouver, British Columbia, thence to Yellowstone National Park and into Utah. After stops at Salt Lake City, Omaha, Chicago, Buffalo, and Boston, Kipling continued to Elmira, New York, for the interview with Mark Twain that is included in this volume. He lingered at Beaver, Pennsylvania, to woo and lose an American maid before proceeding to New York City, where, on September 25, 1889, he boarded the *City of Berlin* for England.

As required by his contract, Kipling regularly mailed letters to India containing his impressions of his four-month sojourn in the United States, and the letters were published in the *Allahabad Pioneer*. Ambitious to get on with his unfolding career as an author, Kipling established himself in England, and by 1891 he had been acknowledged by many critics as Great Britain's "literary man of the hour." At that time he apparently gave little thought to the letters from America that he had composed for the *Pioneer*, regarding them only as the means that enabled him to escape an increasingly repressive environment in India. Therefore, it came as a surprise when during 1891 his letters to the *Allahabad Pioneer* were published under his name as *American Notes* (appropriating the title of Dickens's popular exposé of American life) by the M. J. Ivers Company of New York City.[6]

Other publishers quickly rushed to print with their own editions, and eventually eighteen different editions of *American Notes* were published in the United States. Finally, in 1899, Kipling copyrighted his Allahabad letters, retaining the title *American Notes*, and published them with his collected works, *From Sea to Sea*.

Thus American readers had easy access to abundant, low-priced copies of Kipling's *American Notes* during the 1890s.

[5]Israel Kaplan, "Kipling's First Visit to America," *Dalhousie Review* 39 (Summer, 1959): 160.
[6]Wilson, *The Strange Ride of Rudyard Kipling*, p. 26.

Responses to it varied by region. Westerners denounced Kipling as "that impudent runt" and his work as canard, blasphemy, and scurrilous libel. In an appeal to the editor at Allahabad, Kipling had anticipated this sort of reaction: "Protect me from the wrath of an outraged community if these letters be ever read by American eyes."[7]

While in San Francisco, Kipling had been a guest at the Bohemian Club, a coterie of local writers, artists, playwrights, and musicians. When "the clubmen read what he had written about them" in *American Notes,* "they were aghast, insulted, and incensed," and they missed no opportunity to publish responses. They agreed that Kipling "was always a careless distributor of insult in his writing." Bailey Millard, a San Francisco journalist who had befriended Kipling soon after his arrival, wrote in his review of *American Notes* that Kipling exhibited a "positive genius for reporting the thing which was not." Millard recalled Kipling's attitude in San Francisco as "wondering why the whole world was not ready to rise up and hail him," and he claimed that Kipling was shocked when he departed California that "not a soul in all the Golden State had recognized his genius."[8]

Many western reviewers called Kipling an "inglorious Columbus" who discovered America in 1889 and justified reprinting his works as a way to "get even" for his calumny on their regions; they derived a "certain sweetness of revenge in reading Kipling's *American Notes* in a pirated edition." One reviewer claimed that Kipling arrived in San Francisco "equipped with keen powers of observation, numerous clever and original tricks of expression, and a genuine prejudice against anything American." He added that Kipling was never "hampered by any respect for the facts in the case."[9]

A moderate review of *American Notes* stated, "The only deflection that we have ever observed on Mr. Kipling's part from

[7]Israel Kaplan, "Kipling's *American Notes* and Mark Twain Interview," *Bibliographical Society of America Papers* 44 (1949): 69.

[8]Bailey Millard, "How Kipling Discovered America," *The Bookman* 26 (January, 1908): 483.

[9]McKnight, "Kipling's View of Americans," pp. 132-33.

the requirements of perfect taste and tact, is . . . that portion of his literary work which records his impressions of America and Americans. . . . His impressions and observations should have been set forth with the sobriety and courtesy of a gentleman, and not in the supercilious patter of the cockney."[10]

Reviews favorable to Kipling's *American Notes* were by easterners. One supportive critic explained that Kipling was accustomed to India, where everyone had his social place, and the young writer "was unnerved by the disorderly spectacle of the Western states." Another reviewer chortled, "Those absurd Chicagoans, who had grown so aggressive with their big buildings, their stock yards and their Fair, richly deserve the 'trouncing' Kipling gave them." And a third stated that, when reading *American Notes,* "One is always in the company of a rollicking boy, who . . . is off alone on his first long lark." He asserted that "the letters about Americans are really not so intemperate" as they might seem because "some Americans have peculiar manners, habits of speech, and a mental attitude often objectionable to other Americans and always offensive to foreigners." A Bostonian explained the West's reaction to Kipling's *American Notes* by saying: "They are awfully thin-skinned in the West. Now in Boston it's different. We don't care what the English people think of us."[11]

Reviews of *American Notes* in England varied. One critic characterized Kipling as "not a wise traveler" but rather "a callow and inexperienced globe-trotter when he opened his visit to America by unleashing casual criticisms of the shibboleths of the republic on the California press."[12]

Kipling was twenty-three years old when his ship docked at San Francisco on May 28, 1889. What was he like, this "cynical genius," witting author of the American letters to the *Allahabad Pioneer* but unwitting author of the pirated book *American Notes?*

[10]"Chronicle and Comment," *The Bookman* 5 (March, 1897): 6.

[11]"Review—From Sea to Sea," *The Nation* 69 (September 7, 1899), p. 194; *The New York Times,* June 10, 1899; and Arthur B. Maurice, "Kipling's Men," *The Bookman* 8 (December, 1898): 348.

[12]Martin Fido, *Rudyard Kipling* (New York, 1974), p. 56.

Men at the Bohemian Club recalled that he was a "bronze-featured" little man "with a round head, a good-natured countenance, a sort of cleft chin, a pair of sharp black eyes behind spectacles," who smoked "a perfectly villainous briar-root pipe," and who maintained "the Anglican air of indifference toward everything." To the native westerners he was "the very caricature of the tweed-suited Englishman."[13]

Millard recalled that the visitor was clearly "British and a Tory." Millard introduced Kipling around San Francisco, and he talked with the natives "in a friendly, though somewhat condescending way. But," Millard explained, "we had always looked for this from Englishmen, and did not mind it." Millard recalled that Kipling seemed to respect only two Americans, Bret Harte and Mark Twain, and that he was compulsively opinionated. In conversations he "ventured such opinions upon our undemocratic democracy as would have won him the life-long friendship of Mr. Debs." Millard received the impression that Kipling regarded his visit to San Francisco as a sort of slumming tour; he frequented the Bohemian Club, where the male elite of San Francisco gathered, but he seemed to regard the group as a "curiosity," and he was piqued that "not a soul recognized his genius."[14]

If Americans, particularly Westerners, were indifferent to Kipling's genius, Europeans regarded him otherwise. In 1907 he received the Nobel Prize for Literature, Great Britain's first laureate. The literary bastard *American Notes* drifted about the pirate-publisher underworld for nearly a decade after the Ivers Company fashioned Kipling's letters to the *Allahabad Pioneer* into a book. After copyrighting *American Notes* and publishing it in *From Sea to Sea* in 1899, Kipling authorized several separate editions, including the Books, Inc., Art-Type edition (New York: 1910), which is the basis of this edition. His interview with Mark Twain, absent from the Art-Type edition, is added here to present Kipling's total American experience during 1889.

[13]Kaplan, "Kipling's First Visit to America," p. 160; and Millard, "How Kipling Discovered America," p. 483.
[14]Millard, "How Kipling Discovered America," p. 485.

The primary purpose of this enterprise is to resuscitate *American Notes* and present it as an illuminating treatise on a portion of the American West (most of its content is devoted to the territory west of Omaha) during the late nineteenth century. Beneath the veneer of sneering caricature of westerners, their ways, and institutions is a useful residue of fresh information on regional development.

Perhaps the most intriguing feature of *American Notes* is the direction the narrator took, as if following the return route of Washington Irving's Astorians. Kipling sensed the mind-set of the American track of empire—traditionally east to west. He was amused by the natives' surprise at his countering that flow: they "could not imagine an Englishman coming through the States from West to East instead of by the regularly ordained route." Kipling's itinerary, from the Pacific to the Atlantic, provides a welcome change of narrative direction.

One is struck by the author's devastating candor in declaring his likes and dislikes. He scorned western politics—the Saloon Parliament and politicians—most of whom he claimed were dissolute Irishmen. He belittled western newspapers, whose chauvinistic editors assured their readers that the United States was "the best, finest, bravest, richest, and most progressive nation under Heaven." Western railroads terrified Kipling. The suppressive tunnels and the long, wooden trestles over deep, threatening canyons that trembled under the train's weight made him faint, and he found the cars grossly limited in service and comfort.

He inveighed against the western habit of chewing and spitting tobacco. Westerners "spat on principle." Spittoons were everywhere: in the halls, on the stairs, even in the bedrooms and in "places more sacred than these," meaning, of course, the water closets. Kipling plaintively queried: "Why does the Westerner spit? It can't amuse him, and it doesn't interest his neighbor."

The Englishman was scornful of westerners' values, particularly their pervasive materialism: "The first thing I have been taught to believe is that money is everything in America," and certainly in the West all seemed to be expressed "in dollar terms." He pontificated that this was understandable in "the opening of a new country; but when a man tells you it is civilization, you object. The first thing that the civilized man learns to do is to keep the dollars in the background, because they are only the oil of the machine that makes life go smoothly."

Kipling's likes were more limited. He particularly enjoyed the free lunch served in western saloons. The two American men he liked and respected were Bret Harte and Mark Twain. And he liked a few of the westerners' qualities, particularly their versatility; they were "as cocksure as a man can be." And he had a secret respect for the western spirit, which he interpreted in Darwinian terms: "Recklessness is in the air. . . . The roaring winds off the Pacific make you drunk to begin with." The men who "stocked" the West were "physically, and as far as regards certain tough virtues, the pick of the earth. The inept and the weakly died *en route."*

Above all else, Kipling liked western women and the environment. *American Notes* is laced with rhapsodic utterances about the beauty and charm of American women. During his American tour he fell in love with eight girls and became engaged to one; after losing her, he later wedded another American girl. He exulted that Western women "are very fair . . . of generous build, large, well-groomed," exceeding in beauty the "sweet and comely" maids of Devonshire and the more demure "damsels of France," who clung "closely to their mothers, and with large eyes wondering at the wicked world."

Kipling was no less exultant in his hymns to western vistas: "A very young moon showed herself over a snow-flecked peak. Then the Yellowstone, hidden by the water-willows, lifted up its voice and sang a little song to the mountains." In ecstasy over American nature, the young writer drew exciting metaphors and similes: The Columbia River was "penned between gigantic stone walls crowned with the ruined bastions of Oriental palaces," its course strewn with huge "black-fanged" stones, one of them a "wicked devil's thumb nail of rock shot up a hundred feet in midstream." He adored all of Western nature except the sagebrush: in its "impoverished misery" this plant "is blue, it is stunted, it is dusty. It wraps the rolling hills as a mildewed shroud wraps the body of a long-dead man. It makes you weep for sheer loneliness." Aside from the sage, the Western milieu caused Kipling to conclude: "The American Continent may now sink under the sea, for I have taken the best that it yields, and the best was neither dollars, love, nor real estate."

Associated with Kipling's infatuation with the Western environment was his concern that it be protected: "The great American nation . . . very seldom attempts to put back anything that it has taken from Nature's shelves. It grabs all it can and moves on," but, he admonished, "the grabbing must stop." He regarded control of resource exploitation as a national matter and urged formation of a federal agency to require more prudent use of remaining resources.

Part of the value of *American Notes* is the author's timely arrival in the West: he was a witness to the ending of the old order and the beginning of the new. He saw in the territory between San Francisco and Omaha that the "moving-on is nearly finished," meaning that the frontier processes had about ended. The buffalo had been exterminated. The cowboy, that "picturesque ruffian," was threatened with extinction. Kipling was told: "The cowboy's going under before long. Soon as the country's settled up he'll have to go." The Indian, only recently conquered and festering on bleak reservations or performing as a curiosity in Wild West shows, faced a similar fate. Kipling observed: "Most Americans are charmingly frank about the Indian. 'Let us get rid of him as soon as possible,' they say. 'We have no use for him.'"

The emerging new order, Kipling observed, had in large part been brought about by American enterprise spanning the continent with a grid of railway lines. Besides bringing settlers and goods into the West, the railroads carried many new American characters, including the "commercial traveler" (a euphemism for the drummer of earlier times) and the tourist. Kipling was in daily contact with American tourists. He noted that their sampling of the wonders of the West often began with a journey to Alaska, then to Yosemite, "returning leisurely via the Yellowstone just in time for the tail-end of the summer season at Saratoga." Kipling had some choice comments about tourists and tourist directors, the early-day travel agents. The curse that he placed on tourist directors required that they "die an evil death at the hand of a mad locomotive," and to him tourists were "irreverent Americans" because of the abuse they inflicted on the beauties of nature that he so revered. As Kipling coursed over Yellowstone Park with a party of American tourists, their mindless theft of natural objects and graffiti scrawlings on rock faces amazed him. He expressed relief that, because tourist damage to Yellowstone had been so widespread, the president had ordered the army to guard the park. Cavalry units fresh from campaigns against Geronimo and the Apaches patrolled tourist trails in Yellowstone to keep visitors from bringing up fence-rails to float in the geyser pools, chipping the "fretted tracery of the formations with a geological hammer," or walking onto thin mineral crust, foolishly "cooking" themselves. Also the cavalry patrols watched for poachers, who regularly slipped into the park to shoot bison, deer, elk, and bear.

American Notes is an insult to western Americans, a catalog of ridicule, a regional libel. But it also is a breezy, readable, surprisingly perceptive analysis of a primitive region poised on the threshold of modern times. Rudyard Kipling picked the best possible time to examine the American West.

There was an epilogue to Kipling's 1889 reconnaissance of western America. In 1892 he married Caroline Balestier, sister of his closest friend, Wolcott Balestier, an American writer living in England. That same year the couple settled in Vermont near Brattleboro, where Kipling continued his highly successful literary career. Still, his predeliction for excoriating American society persisted. New York City regularly felt his verbal lash; its people were "barbarians," and the city a "long, narrow pig-trough." Thus it is understandable that he left the United States in 1896, returning with his family to England, where he lived out his life (dying in 1936) as one of the world's most popular writers.[15]

[15]*New York Times,* May 8, 1892; and Howard C. Rice, "Rudyard Kipling in New England," *The New England Quarterly* 9 (September, 1936: 374.

AMERICAN
NOTES

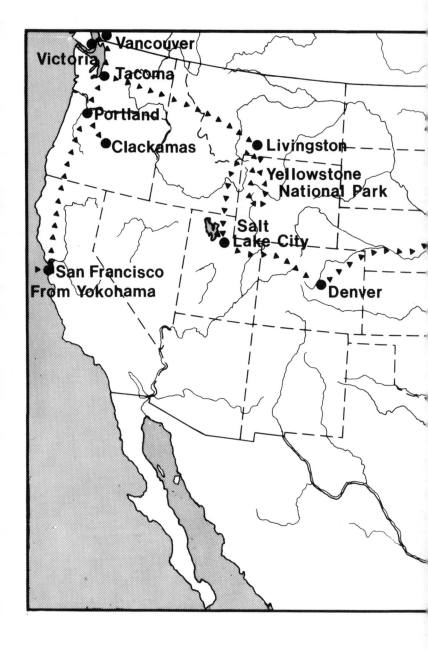

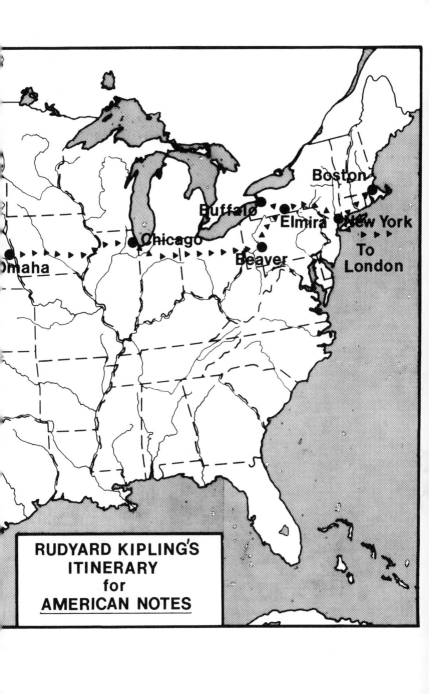

RUDYARD KIPLING'S
ITINERARY
for
AMERICAN NOTES

I

> "Then spoke der Captain Stossenheim
> Who had theories of God,
> 'Oh, Breitmann, this is judgment on
> Der ways dot you have trod.
> You only lifs to enjoy yourself
> While you yourself agree
> Dot self-development requires
> Der religious Idee.'"

This is America. They call her the *City of Peking,*[1] and she belongs to the Pacific Mail Company, but for all practical purposes she is the United States.

We are divided between missionaries and generals—generals who were at Vicksburg and Shiloh,[2] and German by birth, but more American than the Americans, who in confidence tell you

---

[1]The *City of Peking* was a Pacific Mail Line steamer built in the shipyards at Chester, Pennsylvania, in 1874. At the time it was the largest ship in the American merchant service: 423 feet long, 48 feet wide, and 38 feet deep, with a gross tonnage over 5,000 tons and 4,000 horsepower. This vessel, which made the run between San Francisco and Yokohama in a record 15 days, 9 hours, was on the U.S. naval reserve list as a cruiser with armament of six 5-inch "quickfirers" and eight machine guns.

[2]Vicksburg in western Mississippi was the site of a bloody Civil War siege from November, 1862, to July, 1863, applied by a large Union army on Confederate defenders to gain control of the Mississippi River. The ultimate Confederate capitulation opened the Mississippi River to Union operations and sundered the Confederacy. Shiloh in Hardin County, Tennessee, was the site of one of the bloodiest engagements of the Civil War, also called the Battle of Pittsburg Landing. Confederate forces appeared to have triumphed by forcing the Union retreat, but, lacking reinforcements, the Confederates withdrew, providing in the long run a Union victory.

that they are not generals at all, but only brevet[3] majors of militia corps. The missionaries are perhaps the queerest portion of the cargo.[4] Did you ever hear an English minister lecture for half an hour on the freight-traffic receipts and general working of, let us say, the Midland? The Professor has been sitting at the feet of a keen-eyed, close-bearded, swarthy man who expounded unto him kindered mysteries with a fluency and precision that a city leader-writer might have envied. "Who's your financial friend with the figures at his fingers' ends?" I asked. "Missionary—Presbyterian Mission to the Japs," said the professor. I laid my hand upon my mouth and was dumb.

As a counterpose to the missionaries, we carry men from Manila—lean Scotchmen who gamble once a month in the Manila State lottery and occasionally turn up trumps. One, at least, drew a ten-thousand-dollar prize last December and is away to make merry in the New World. Everybody on the staff of an American steamer this side the Continent seems to gamble steadily in that lottery, and the talk of the smoking-room runs almost entirely on prizes won by accident or lost through a moment's delay. The tickets are sold more or less openly at Yokohama and Hong-Kong, and the drawings—losers and winners both agree here—are above reproach.

We have resigned ourselves to the infinite monotony of a twenty days' voyage. The Pacific Mail advertises falsely. Only under the most favorable circumstances of wind and steam can their under-engined boats cover the distance in fifteen days. Our *City of Peking,* for instance, had been jogging along at a gentle ten knots an hour, a pace out of all proportion to her bulk. "When we get a

[3]The brevet rank was widely used by the U.S. Army in the nineteenth century to promote an officer to a higher rank, often without increased pay. It was also a temporary command rank.

[4]Beginning in the late nineteenth century American Protestant and Roman Catholic missionary societies found China and Japan attractive fields for mission work, establishing schools and churches and converting the people. The missionaries herein referred to would be a shuttle group returning to the United States for furlough and to raise funds among American churches to continue the Far Eastern work.

wind," says the Captain, "we shall do better." She is a four-master and can carry any amount of canvas. It is not safe to run steamers across this void under the poles of Atlantic liners. The monotony of the sea is paralyzing. We have passed the wreck of a little sealing-schooner lying bottom up and covered with gulls. She weltered by in the chill dawn, unlovely as the corpse of a man; and the wild birds piped thinly at us as they steered her across the surges. The pulse of the Pacific is no little thing even in the quieter moods of the sea. It set our bows swinging and nosing and ducking ere we were a day clear of Yokohama, and yet there was never swell nor crested wave in sight. "We ride very high," said the Captain, "and she's a dry boat. She has a knack of crawling over things somehow; but we shan't need to put her to the test this journey."

*

The Captain was mistaken. For four days we have endured the sullen displeasure of the North Pacific, winding up with a night of discomfort. It began with a gray sea, flying clouds, and a head-wind that smote fifty knots off the day's run. Then rose from the southeast a beam sea warranted by no wind that was abroad upon the waters in our neighborhood, and we wallowed in the trough of it for sixteen mortal hours. In the stillness of the harbor, when the newspaper man is lunching in her saloon and the steam-launch is crawling round her sides, a ship of pride is a "stately liner." Out in the open, one rugged shoulder of a sea between you and the horizon, she becomes "the old hooker," a "lively boat," and other things of small import, for this is necessary to propitiate the Ocean. "There's a storm to the southeast of us," explained the Captain. "That's what's kicking up this sea."

The *City of Peking* did not belie her reputation. She crawled over the seas in liveliest wise, never shipping a bucket till—she was forced to. Then she took it green over the bows to the vast edification of, at least, one passenger who had never seen the scuppers full before.

Later in the day the fun began. "Oh, she's a daisy at rolling" murmured the chief steward, flung star-fish-wise on a table among his glassware. "She's rolling some," said a black apparition new risen from the stoke-hold. "Is she going to roll any more?" demanded the ladies grouped in what ought to have been the ladies' saloon, but, according to American custom, was labeled "Social Hall."

Passed in the twilight the chief officer—a dripping, bearded face. "Shall I mark out the bull-board?" said he, and lurched aft, followed by the tongue of a wave. "She'll roll her guards under to-night," said a man from Louisiana, where their river-steamers do not understand the meaning of bulwarks. We dined to a dashing accompaniment of crockery, the bounds of emancipated beer-bottles livelier than their own corks, and the clamor of the ship's gong broken loose and calling to meals on its own account.

After dinner the real rolling began. She did roll "guards under," as the Louisiana man had prophesied. At thirty-minute intervals to the second arrived one big sea, when the electric lamps died down to nothing, and the screw raved and the blows of the sea made the decks quiver. On those occasions we moved from our chairs, not gently, but discourteously. At other times we were merely holding on with both hands.

It was then that I studied Fear—Terror bound in black silk and fighting hard with herself. For reasons which will be thoroughly understood, there was a tendency among the passengers to herd together and to address inquiries to every officer who happened to stagger through the saloon. No one was in the least alarmed, —oh dear, no,—but all were keenly anxious for information. This anxiety redoubled after a more than usually vicious roll. Terror was a large, handsome, and cultured lady who knew the precise value of human life, the inwardness of *Robert Elsmere,* the latest poetry—everything in fact that a clever woman should know.[5] When the rolling was near its worst, she began to talk swiftly. I do not for a moment believe that she knew what she was talking about. The rolling increased. She buckled down to the task of

[5]Mary Augusta Arnold (Mrs. Humphrey Ward), *Robert Ellsmere* (London: Smith and Elder, 1888).

making conversation. By the heave of the laboring bust, the rest-less working of the fingers on the tablecloth, and the uncontrol-lable eyes that turned always to the companion stairhead, I was able to judge the extremity of her fear. Yet her words were frivo-lous and commonplace enough; they poured forth unceasingly, punctuated with little laughs and giggles, as a woman's speech should be. Presently, a member of her group suggested going to bed. No, she wanted to sit up; she wanted to go on talking, and as long as she could get a soul to sit with her she had her desire. When for sheer lack of company she was forced to get to her cabin, she left reluctantly, looking back to the well-lighted saloon over her shoulder. The contrast between the flowing triviality of her speech and the strained intentness of eye and hand was a quaint thing to behold. I know now how Fear should be painted.

No one slept very heavily that night. Both arms were needed to grip the berth, while the trunks below wound the carpet slips into knots and battered the framing of the cabins. Once it seemed to me that the whole of the laboring fabric that cased our trumpery fortunes stood on end and in this undignified posture hopped a mighty hop. Twice I know I shot out of my berth to join the adventurous trunks on the floor. A hundred times the crash of the wave on the ship's side was followed by the roar of the water; as it swept the decks and raved round the deckhouses. In a lull I heard the flying feet of a man, a shout, and a far-away chorus of lost spirits singing somebody's requiem.

May 24 (Queen's Birthday).—If ever you meet an American, be good to him. This day the ship was dressed with flags from stem to stern, and chiefest of the bunting was the Union-Jack. They had given no word of warning to the English, who were proportion-ately pleased. At dinner up rose an ex-Commissioner of the Luck-now Division (on my honor, Anglo-India extends to the ends of the earth!) and gave us the health of Her Majesty and the Presi-dent. It was afterwards that the trouble began. A small American penned half a dozen English into a corner and lectured them soundly on—their want of patriotism!

"What sort of Queen's Birthday do you call this?" he thundered. "What did you drink the President's health for? What's the President to you on this day of all others? Well, suppose you *are* in the minority, all the more reason for standing by your country. Don't talk to me. You Britishers made a mess of it—a mighty bungle of the whole thing. I'm an American of the Americans; but if no one can propose Her Majesty's health better than by just throwing it at your heads, I'm going to try."

Then and there he delivered a remarkably neat little oration— pat, well put together, and clearly delivered. So it came to pass that the Queen's health was best honored by an American. We English were dazed. I wondered how many Englishmen not trained to addressing their fellows would have spoken half so fluently as the gentleman from 'Frisco.

"Well, you see," said one of us feebly, "she's our Queen, any-how and—and—she's been ours for fifty years, and not one of us here has seen England for seven years, and we can't enthuse over the matter. We've lived to be hauled over the coals for want of patriotism by an American! We'll be more careful next time."

And the conversation drifted naturally into the question of the government of men—English, Japanese (we have several traveled Japanese aboard), and Americans throwing the ball from one to another. We bore in mind the golden rule: "Never agree with a man who abuses his own country," and got on well enough.

"Japan," said a little gentleman who was a rich man there, "Japan is divided into two administrative sides. On the one the remains of a very strict and quite oriental despotism; on the other a mass of—what do you call it?—red-tapeism which is not under-stood even by the officials who handle it. We copy the red tape, and when it is copied we believe that we administer. That is a vice of all Oriental nations. We are Orientals."

"Oh, no, say the most westerly of the westerns," purred an American, soothingly.

The little man was pleased. "Thanks. That is what we hope to believe, but up to the present it is not so. Look now. A farmer in my country holds a hillside cut into little terraces. Every year he must submit to his Government a statement of the size and revenue paid, not on the whole hillside, but on each terrace. The complete statement makes a pile three inches high, and is of no use when it is made except to keep in work thousands of officials to check the returns. Is that administration? By God! we call it so, but we multiply officials by the twenty, and they are not administration. What country is such a fool? Look at our Government offices eaten up with clerks! Some day, I tell you, there will be a smash."

This was new to me, but I might have guessed it. In every country where swords and uniforms accompany civil office there is a natural tendency towards an ill-considered increase of officialdom.

"You might pay India a visit some day," I said. "I fancy that you would find that our country shares your trouble."

Thereupon a Japanese gentleman in the Educational Department began to cross-question me on the matters of his craft in India, and in a quarter of an hour got from me the very little that I knew about primary schools, higher education, and the value of an M. A. degree. He knew exactly what he wanted to ask, and only dropped me when the tooth of desire had clean picked the bone of ignorance.

Then an American held forth, harping on a string that has already too often twanged in my ear. "What will it be in America itself?"

"The whole system is rotten from top to bottom," he said. "As rotten as rotten can be."

"That's so," said the Louisiana man, with an affirmative puff of smoke.

"They call us a Republic. We may be. I don't think it. You Britishers have got the only republic worth the name. You choose to run your ship of state with a gilt figurehead; but I know, and so does every man who has thought about it, that your Queen doesn't cost you one-half what our system of pure democracy costs us. Politics in America? There aren't any. The whole question of the day is spoils. That's all. We fight our souls out over tram-contracts, gas-contracts, road-contracts, and any darned thing that will turn a dishonest dollar, and we call that politics. No one but a low-down man will run for Congress and the Senate— the Senate of the freest people on earth are bound slaves to some blessed monopoly. If I had money enough, I could buy the Senate of the United States, the Eagle, and the Star-Spangled Banner complete."

"And the Irish vote included?" said some one—a Britisher, I fancy.

"Certainly, if I chose to go yahooing down the street at the tail of the British lion. Anything dirty will buy the Irish vote. That's why our politics are dirty. Some day you Britishers will grant Home Rule to the vermin in our blankets. Then the real Americans will invite the Irish to get up and git to where they came from. 'Wish you'd hurry up that time before we have another trouble. We're bound hand and foot by the Irish vote; or at least that's the excuse for any unusual theft that we perpetrate. I tell you there's no good in an Irishman except as a fighter. He doesn't understand work. He has a natural gift of the gab, and he can drink a man blind. These three qualifications make him a first-class politician."

With one accord the Americans present commenced to abuse Ireland and its people as they had met them, and each man prefaced his commination service with: "I am an American by birth—an American from way back."

It must be an awful thing to live in a country where you have to explain that you really belong there. Louder grew the clamor and crisper the sentiments.

"If we weren't among Americans, I should say we were consorting with Russians," said a fellow-countryman in my ear.

"They can't mean what they say," I whispered. "Listen to this fellow."

"And I know, for I have been three times round the world and resided in most countries on the Continent, that there was never people yet could govern themselves."

"Allah! This from an American!"

"And who should know better than an American?" was the retort. "For the ignorant—that is to say for the majority—there is only one argument—fear; the fear of Death. In our case we give any scallawag who comes across the water all the same privileges that we have made for ourselves. There we make a mistake. They thank us by playing the fool. Then we shoot them down. You can't persuade the mob of any country to become decent citizens. If they misbehave themselves, shoot them. I saw the bombs thrown at Chicago when our police were blown to bits.[6] I saw the banners in the procession that threw the bombs. All the mottoes on them were in German. The men were aliens in our midst, and they were shot down like dogs. I've been in labor riots and seen the militia go through a crowd like a finger through tissue paper."

"I was in the riots at New Orleans,"[7] said the man from Louisiana. "We turned the Gatling on the other crowd, and they were sick."[8]

"Whew! I wonder what would have happened if a Gatling had been used when the West End riots were in full swing?" said an Englishman. "If a single rioter were killed in an English town by the police, the chances are that the policeman would have to stand his trial for murder and the ministry of the day would go out."

"Then you've got all your troubles before you. The more power you give the people, the more trouble they will give. With us our better classes are corrupt and our lower classes are lawless. There are millions of useful, law-abiding citizens, and they are very sick of this thing. We execute our justice in the streets. The law courts are no use. Take the case of the Chicago Anarchists. It was all we could do to get 'em hanged; whereas the dead in the streets

[6]The Haymarket Square Riot erupted in Chicago on May 4, 1886. Workers' agitation for an eight-hour day and for other improvements in their welfare was taken up by anarchists. A protest group of 1,500 gathered in Haymarket Square. When police attempted to disperse them, a bomb exploded killing eleven, including seven policemen, and wounding over 100. Eight anarchists were arrested, tried, and convicted for the bombing; four persons were hanged.

[7]The New Orleans riots in 1866, were outbursts by Confederate veterans contesting the loss of their voting rights and the enfranchisement of blacks. Thirty-four blacks were slain, and over two hundred were wounded.

[8]The Gatling was a multiple-firing gun, precursor of the machine gun, invented by Richard Jordan Gatling in 1862 and adopted by the U.S. Army in 1866.

had been punished offhand. We were sure of *them*. Guess that's the reason we are so quick to fire on a mob. But it's unfair, all the same. We receive all these cattle—Anarchists, Socialists, and ruffians of every sort—and then we shoot them. The States are as republican as they make 'em. We have no use for a man who wants to try any more experiments on the Constitution. We are the biggest people on God's earth. All the world knows that. We've been shouting that we are also the greatest people. No one cares to contradict us but ourselves; and we are now wondering whether we are what we claim to be. Never mind; you Britishers will have the same experiences to go through. You're beginning to rot now. Your County Councils will make you more rotten because you are putting power into the hands of untrained people. When you reach our level,—every man with a vote and the right to sell it; the right to nominate fellows of his own kidney to swamp out better men,—you'll be what we are now—rotten, rotten, rotten!"

The voice ceased, and no man rose up to contradict.

"We'll worry through it somehow," said the man from Louisiana. "What would do us a world of good now would be a big European war. We're getting slack and sprawly. Now a war outside our borders would make us all pull together. But that's a luxury we shan't get."

"Can't you raise one within your own borders?" I said flippantly, to get rid of the thought of the great blind nation in her unrest putting out her hand to the Sword. Mine was a most unfortunate remark.

"I hope not," said an American, very seriously. "We have paid a good deal to keep ourselves together before this, and it is not likely that we shall split up without protest. Yet some say that we are too large, and some say that Washington and the Eastern States are running the whole country. If ever we do divide,—God help us when we do,—it will be East and West this time."

"We built the old hooker too long in the run. Put the engine-room aft. Break her back," said an American who had not yet spoken. "'Wonder if our forbears knew how she was going to grow."

"A very large country." The speaker sighed as though the weight of it from New York to 'Frisco lay upon his shoulders. "If ever we do divide, it means we are done for. There is no room for four first-class empires in the States. One split will lead to another if the first is successful. What's the use of talking?"

What's the use? Here's our conversation as it ran, the night of the Queen's Birthday. What do *you* think?

II

"Serene, indifferent to fate,
Thou sittest at the western gate,
Thou seest the white seas fold their tents,
Oh warder of two Continents.
Thou drawest all things small and great
To thee beside the Western Gate."

This is what Bret Harte has written of the great city of San Francisco, and for the past fortnight I have been wondering what made him do it.[1]

There is neither serenity nor indifference to be found in these parts; and evil would it be for the Continent whose wardship were intrusted to so reckless a guardian.

Behold me pitched neck-and-crop from twenty days of the High Seas, into the whirl of California, deprived of any guidance, and left to draw my own conclusions. Protect me from the wrath of an outraged community if these letters be ever read by American eyes. San Francisco is a mad city—inhabited for the most part by perfectly insane people whose women are of a remarkable beauty.

When the *City of Peking* steamed through the Golden Gate I saw with great joy that the blockhouse which guarded the mouth of the "finest harbor in the world, Sir," could be silenced by

[1]The American writer Bret Harte was born in Albany, New York, in 1836. He ventured to California as a goldseeker and became a teacher and itinerant journalist. He edited the *Overland Monthly*. His best-known writings are "The Luck of Roaring Camp" and "The Outcasts of Poker Flat."

two gun-boats from Hong-Kong with safety, comfort, and despatch.

Then a reporter leaped aboard, and ere I could gasp held me in his toils. He pumped me exhaustively while I was getting ashore, demanding, of all things in the world, news about Indian journalism. It is an awful thing to enter a new land with a new lie on your lips. I spoke the truth to the evil-minded Customhouse man who turned my most sacred raiment on a floor composed of stable-refuse and pine-splinters; but the reporter overwhelmed me not so much by his poignant audacity as his beautiful ignorance. I am sorry now that I did not tell him more lies as I passed into a city of three hundred thousand white men. Think of it! Three hundred thousand white men and women gathered in one spot, walking upon real pavements in front of real plate-glass windowed shops, and talking something that was not very different from English. It was only when I had tangled myself up in a hopeless maze of small wooden houses, dust, street-refuse, and children who play with empty kerosene tins, that I discovered the difference of speech.

"You want to go to the Palace Hotel?" said an affable youth on a dray. "What in hell are you doing here, then? This is about the lowest place in the city. Go six blocks north to the corner of Geary and Market; then walk around till you strike corner of Gutter and Sixteenth, and that brings you there."[2]

I do not vouch for the literal accuracy of these directions, quoting but from a disordered memory.

"Amen," I said. "But who am I that I should strike the corners of such as you name? Peradventure they be gentlemen of repute, and might hit back. Bring it down to dots, my son."

I thought he would have smitten me, but he didn't. He explained that no one ever used the word "street," and that every one was supposed to know how the streets run: for sometimes

[2]By Gutter Street, Kipling meant Sutter Street, named for John August Sutter, a northern California pioneer. This is Kipling's error rather than the typesetter's because this spelling appears in other editions of *American Notes* which Kipling personally examined for revision.

the names were upon the lamps and sometimes they weren't. Fortified with these directions I proceeded till I found a mighty street full of sumptuous buildings four or five stories high, but paved with rude cobble-stones in the fashion of the Year One. A cable-car without any visible means of support slid stealthily behind me and nearly struck me in the back. A hundred yards further there was a slight commotion in the street—a gathering together of three or four—and something glittered as it moved very swiftly. A ponderous Irish gentleman with priest's cords in his hat and a small nickel-plated badge on his fat bosom emerged from the knot, supporting a Chinaman who had been stabbed in the eye and was bleeding like a pig. The bystanders went their ways, and the Chinaman, assisted by the policeman, his own. Of course this was none of my business, but I rather wanted to know what had happened to the gentleman who had dealt the stab. It said a great deal for the excellence of the municipal arrangements of the town that a surging crowd did not at once block the street to see what was going forward. I was the sixth man and the last who assisted at the performance, and my curiosity was six times the greatest. Indeed, I felt ashamed of showing it.

There were no more incidents till I reached the Palace Hotel, a seven-storied warren of humanity with a thousand rooms in it. All the travel-books will tell you about hotel arrangements in this country. They should be seen to be appreciated. Understand clearly—and this letter is written after a thousand miles of experiences—that money will not buy you service in the West.

When the hotel clerk—the man who awards your room to you and who is supposed to give you information—when that resplendent individual stoops to attend to your wants, he does so whistling or humming, or picking his teeth, or pauses to converse with some one he knows. These performances, I gather, are to impress upon you that he is a free man and your equal. From his general appearance and the size of his diamonds he ought to be your superior. There is no necessity for this swaggering self-consciousness of freedom. Business is business, and the man who is paid to attend to a man might reasonably devote his whole attention to the job.

In a vast marble-paved hall under the glare of an electric light sat forty or fifty men; and for their use and amusement were provided spittoons of infinite capacity and generous gape. Most of the men wore frock-coats and top-hats,—the things that we in India put on at a wedding breakfast if we possessed them,—but they all spat. They spat on principle. The spittoons were on the staircases, in each bedroom—yea, and in chambers even more sacred than these. They chased one into retirement, but they blossomed in chiefest splendor round the Bar, and they were all used, every reeking one of 'em.

Just before I began to feel deathly sick, another reporter grappled me. What he wanted to know was the precise area of India in square miles. I referred him to Whittaker. He had never heard of Whittaker. He wanted it from my own mouth, and I would not tell him. Then he swerved off, like the other man, to details of journalism in our own country. I ventured to suggest that the interior economy of a paper most concerned the people who worked it. "That's the very thing that interests us," he said. "Have you got reporters anything like our reporters on Indian newspapers?" "We have not," I said, and suppressed the "Thank God" rising to my lips. "*Why* haven't you?" said he. "Because they would die," I said. It was exactly like talking to a child— a very rude little child. He would begin almost every sentence with: "Now tell me something about India," and would turn aimlessly from one question to another without the least continuity. I was not angry, but keenly interested. The man was a revelation to me. To his questions I returned answers mendacious and evasive. After all, it really did not matter what I said. He could not understand. I can only hope and pray that none of the readers of the *Pioneer* will ever see that portentous interview.[3] The man made me out to be an idiot several sizes more driveling than my destiny intended, and the rankness of his ignorance managed to distort the few poor facts with which I supplied him into large

---

[3]The *Allahabad Pioneer* was Kipling's paper in India, which commissioned him to travel to the United States and prepare feature articles for its readers.

and elaborate lies. Then thought I: "The matter of American journalism shall be looked into later on. At present I will enjoy myself."

No man rose to tell me what were the lions of the place. No one volunteered any sort of conveyance. I was absolutely alone in this big city of white folk. By instinct I sought refreshment and came upon a barroom, full of bad Salon pictures, in which men with hats on the backs of their heads were wolfing food from a counter. It was the institution of the "Free Lunch" that I had struck. You paid for a drink and got as much as you wanted to eat. For something less than a rupee a day a man can feed himself sumptuously in San Francisco, even though he be bankrupt. Remember this if ever you are stranded in these parts.

Later, I began a vast but unsystematic exploration of the streets. I asked for no names. It was enough that the pavements were full of white men and women, the streets clanging with traffic, and that the restful roar of a great city rang in my ears. The cable cars glided to all points of the compass. I took them one by one till I could go no farther. San Francisco has been pitched down on the sand bunkers of the Bikaneer desert. About one-fourth of it is ground reclaimed from the sea—any old-timer will tell you all about that. The remainder is ragged, unthrifty sandhills, pegged down by houses.

From an English point of view there has not been the least attempt at grading those hills, and indeed you might as well try to grade the hillocks of Sind. The cable-cars have for all practical purposes made San Francisco a dead level. They take no count of rise or fall, but slide equably on their appointed courses from one end to the other of a six-mile street. They turn corners almost at right angles; cross other lines, and, for aught I know, may run up the sides of houses. There is no visible agency of their flight; but once in a while you shall pass a five-storied building, humming with machinery that winds up an everlasting wire-cable, and the initiated will tell you that here is the mechanism. I gave up asking questions. If it pleases Providence to make a car run up and down a slit in the ground for many miles, and if for twopence-halfpenny I can ride in that car, why shall I seek the reasons of the miracle? Rather let me look out of the windows till the shops give place to thousands and thousands of little houses made of wood—each house just big enough for a man and his family. Let me watch the people in the cars, and try to find out in what manner they differ from us, their ancestors.

They delude themselves into the belief that they talk English, —*the* English,—and I have already been pitied for speaking with "an English Accent." The man who pitied me spoke, so far as I was concerned, the language of thieves. And they all do. Where we put the accent forward, they throw it back, and *vice versa;* where we use the long *a,* they use the short; and words so simple as to be past mistaking, they pronounce somewhere up in the dome of their heads. How do these things happen?

Oliver Wendell Holmes says that Yankee schoolmarms, the cider, and the salt codfish of the Eastern States are responsible for what he calls a nasal accent. A Hindu is a Hindu, and a brother to the man who knows his vernacular; and a Frenchman is French because he speaks his own language; but the American has no language. He is dialect, slang, provincialism, accent, and so forth. Now that I have heard their voices, all the beauty of Bret Harte is being ruined for me, because I find myself catching through the roll of his rhythmical prose the cadence of his peculiar fatherland. Get an American lady to read to you "How Santa Claus came to Simpson's Bar," and see how much is, under her tongue, left of the beauty of the original.[4]

But I am sorry for Bret Harte. It happened this way. A reporter asked me what I thought of the city, and I made answer suavely that it was hallowed ground to me because of Bret Harte. That was true.

"Well," said the reporter, "Bret Harte claims California, but California don't claim Bret Harte. He's been so long in England that he's quite English. Have you seen our cracker-factories and the new offices of the *Examiner*?"[5] He could not understand that

[4]"How Santa Claus Came to Simpson's Bar," from Bret Harte, *Tales of the Argonauts and in the Hollow of the Hills and Other Tales* (Boston: Houghton Mifflin Company, 1921), 3: 66-83.

to the outside world the city was worth a great deal less than the man.

*

Night fell over the Pacific, and the white sea-fog whipped through the streets, dimming the splendors of the electric lights. It is the use of this city, her men and women, to parade between the hours of eight and ten a certain street, called Kearney Street, where the finest shops are situated. Here the click of heels on the pavement is loudest, here the lights are brightest, and here the thunder of the traffic is most overwhelming. I watched Young California and saw that it was at least expensively dressed, cheerful in manner, and self-asserting in conversation. Also the women are very fair. The maidens were of generous build, large, well-groomed, and attired in raiment that even to my inexperienced eyes must have cost much. Kearney Street, at nine o'clock, levels all distinctions of rank as impartially as the grave.[6] Again and again I loitered at the heels of a couple of resplendent beings, only to overhear, when I expected the level voice of culture, the *staccato* "Sez he," "Sez I," that is the mark of the white servant-girl all the world over.

This was depressing because, in spite of all that goes to the contrary, fine feathers ought to make fine birds. There was wealth —unlimited wealth—in the streets, but not an accent that would have been dear at fifty cents. Wherefore, revolving in my mind that these folk were barbarians, I was presently enlightened and made aware that they also were the heirs of all the ages, and civilized after all. There appeared before me an affable stranger of prepossessing appearance, with a blue and an innocent eye. Addressing me by name, he claimed to have met me in New

[5]The *San Francisco Examiner,* one of the city's oldest surviving newspapers.

[6]Kearney Street is Kearny Street, named for General Stephen Watts Kearny, Commander of the Army of the West, the United States invasion force in Mexican territory in the Southwest (New Mexico, Arizona, and California); and military governor of California.

York at the Windsor, and to this claim I gave a qualified assent. I did not remember the fact, but since he was so certain of it, why then—I waited developments.

"And what did you think of Indiana when you came through?" was the next question.

It revealed the mystery of previous acquaintance, and one or two other things. With reprehensible carelessness, my friend of the light-blue eye had looked up the name of his victim in the hotel register and read "India" for Indiana.

He could not imagine an Englishman coming through the States from West to East instead of by the regularly ordained route. My fear was that in his delight at finding me so responsive he would make remarks about New York and the Windsor which I could not understand. And indeed, he adventured in this direction once or twice, asking me what I thought of such and such streets, which, from his tone, I gathered were anything but respectable. It is trying to talk unknown New York in almost unknown San Francisco. But my friend was merciful. He protested that I was one after his own heart, and pressed upon me rare and curious drinks at more than one bar. These drinks I accepted with gratitude, as also the cigars with which his pockets were stored. He would show me the Life of the city. Having no desire to watch a weary old play again, I evaded the offer, and received in lieu of the Devil's instruction much coarse flattery. Curiously constituted is the soul of man. Knowing how and where this man lied; waiting idly for the finale; I was distinctly conscious, as he bubbled compliments in my ear, of soft thrills of gratified pride. I was wise quoth he, anybody could see that with half an eye; sagacious; versed in the affairs of the world; an acquaintance to be desired; one who had tasted the cup of Life with discretion.

All this pleased me, and in a measure numbed the suspicion that was thoroughly aroused. Eventually the blue-eyed one discovered, nay insisted, that I had a taste for cards (this was clumsily worked in, but it was my fault, in that I met him half-way, and allowed him no chance of good acting). Hereupon, I laid my head to one side, and simulated unholy wisdom, quoting odds and ends of poker-talk, all ridiculously misapplied. My friend kept his countenance admirably; and well he might, for five minutes later we arrived, always by the purest of chances, at a place where we could play cards, and also frivol with Louisiana State Lottery tickets. Would I play?

"Nay," said I, "for to me cards have neither meaning nor continuity; but let us assume that I am going to play. How would you and your friends get to work? Would you play a straight game or make me drunk, or—well, the fact is I'm a newspaper man, and I'd be much obliged if you'd let me know something about bunco-steering."

My blue-eyed friend cursed me by his gods,—the Right and Left Bower; he even cursed the very good cigars he had given me. But, the storm over, he quieted down and explained. I apologized for causing him to waste an evening, and we spent a very pleasant time together.

Inaccuracy, provincialism, and a too hasty rushing to conclusions were the rocks that he had split on; but he got his revenge when he said:

"How would I play with you? From all the poppycock" (*Anglice,* bosh) "you talked about poker, I'd ha' played a straight game and skinned you. I wouldn't have taken the trouble to make you drunk. You never knew anything of the game; but the way I was mistaken in you makes me sick."

He glared at me as though I had done him an injury. To-day I know how it is that, year after year, week after week, the bunco-steerer, who is the confidence-trick and the card-sharper of other climes, secures his prey. He slavers them with flattery, as the snake slavers the rabbit. The incident depressed me because it showed I had left the innocent East far behind, and was come to a country where a man must look out for himself. The very hotel glistened with notices about keeping my door locked, and depositing my valuables in a safe. The white man in a lump is bad. Weeping softly for O-Toyo (little I knew then that my heart was to be torn afresh from my bosom!), I fell asleep in the clanging hotel.[7]

[7]O-Toyo was one of many women Kipling encountered on his journey from India to England via the Far East and the United States. He met

Next morning I had entered upon the Deferred Inheritance. There are no princes in America,—at least with crowns on their heads,—but a generous-minded member of some royal family received my letter of introduction. Ere the day closed I was a member of the two clubs and booked for many engagements to dinner and party. Now this prince, upon whose financial operations be continual increase, had no reason, nor had the others, his friends, to put himself out for the sake of one Briton more or less; but he rested not till he had accomplished all in my behalf that a mother could think of for her *débutante* daughter. Do you know the Bohemian Club of San Francisco?[8] They say its fame extends over the world. It was created somewhat on the lines of the Savage by men who wrote or drew things, and it has blossomed into most unrepublican luxury. The ruler of the place is an owl—an owl standing upon a skull and crossbones, showing forth grimly the wisdom of the man of letters and the end of his hopes for immortality. The owl stands on the staircase, a statue four feet high, is carved in the woodwork, flutters on the frescoed ceilings, is stamped on the note-paper, and hangs on the walls. He is an Ancient and Honorable Bird. Under his wing 'twas my privilege to meet with white men whose lives were not chained down to routine of toil, who wrote magazine articles instead of reading them hurriedly in the pauses of office-work, who painted pictures instead of contenting themselves with cheap etchings picked up at another man's sale of effects. Mine were all the rights of social intercourse that India, stony-hearted stepmother of Collectors, has swindled us out of. Treading soft carpets and breathing the incense of superior cigars, I wandered from room

---

O-Toyo in a Nagasaki tea garden. Kipling lamented: "O-Toyo, Ebon-haired, rosy cheeked, and made throughout of delicate porcelain. I have left my heart with O-Toyo under the Pines."

[8]The Bohemian Club was organized in March, 1872, in San Francisco by writers, actors, artists, and journalists of the city. Ambrose Bierce and John C. Cremony were charter members, and Henry George was elected to the first board of trustees. Two of the most sought-after persons withdrew because they objected to the name Bohemian. Evenings at the Bohemian Club included debates, poetry, and plays.

to room studying the paintings in which the members of the Club had caricatured themselves, their associates, and their aims. There was a slick French audacity about the workmanship of these men of toil unbending that went straight to the heart of the beholder. And yet it was not altogether French. A dry grimness of treatment, almost Dutch, marked the difference. The men painted as they spoke—with certainty. The club indulges in revelries which it calls "jinks"—high and low,—at intervals,—and each of these gatherings is faithfully portrayed in oils by hands that know their business. In this club were no amateurs spoiling canvas because they fancied they could handle oils without knowledge of shadows or anatomy—no gentleman of leisure ruining the temper of publishers and an already ruined market with attempts to write "because everybody writes something these days."

My hosts were working, or had worked, for their daily bread with pen or paint, and their talk for the most part was of the shop shoppy—that is to say, delightful. They extended a large hand of welcome and were as brethren, and I did homage to the Owl and listened to their talk. An Indian Club about Christmastime will yield, if properly worked, an abundant harvest of queer tales; but at a gathering of Americans from the uttermost ends of their own continent the tales are larger, thicker, more spinous, and even more azure than any Indian variety. Tales of the War I heard told by an ex-officer of the South over his evening drink to a Colonel of the Northern army; my introducer, who had served as a trooper in the Northern Horse, throwing in emendations from time to time.

Other voices followed with equally wondrous tales of riata-throwing in Mexico or Arizona, of gambling at army posts in Texas, or newspaper wars waged in godless Chicago, of deaths sudden and violent in Montana and Dakota, of the loves of half-breed maidens in the South, and fantastic huntings for gold in mysterious Alaska. Above all, they told the story of the building of old San Francisco, when the "finest collection of humanity on God's earth, Sir, started this town, and the water came up to the foot of Market Street." Very terrible were some of the tales, grimly humorous the others, and the men in broadcloth and fine linen who told them had played their parts in them.

"And now and again when things got too bad they would toll the city bell, and the Vigilance Committee turned out and hanged the suspicious characters. A man didn't begin to be suspected in those days till he had committed at least one unprovoked murder," said a calm-eyed, portly old gentleman.[9]

I looked at the pictures around me; the noiseless, neat-uniformed waiter behind me, the oak-ribbed ceiling above, the velvety carpet beneath. It was hard to realize that even twenty years ago you could see a man hanged with great pomp. Later on I found reason to change my opinion. The tales gave me a headache and set me thinking. How in the world was it possible to take in even one-thousandth of this huge, roaring, many sided continent? In the silence of the sumptuous library lay Professor Bryce's book on the American Republic.[10]

"It is an omen," said I. "He has done all things in all seriousness, and he may be purchased for half a guinea. Those who desire information of the most undoubted must refer to his pages. For me is the daily round of vagabondage, the recording of the incidents of the hour, and talk with the traveling companion of the day. I will not 'do' this country at all."

And I forgot all about India for ten days while I went out to dinners and watched the social customs of the people, which are entirely different from our customs, and was introduced to the men of many millions. These persons are harmless in their earlier stages; that is to say, a man worth three or four million dollars may be a good talker, clever, amusing and of the world; a man with twice that amount is to be avoided; and a twenty-million man is—just twenty millions. Take an instance. I was speaking to a newspaper man about seeing the proprietor of his journal. My friend snorted indignantly:

[9]Soon after the Gold Rush of 1849, San Francisco became as notorious as the Barbary Coast because lawlessness flourished. Local citizens organized the San Francisco Vigilance Committee, which functioned for some time as an extra-legal agency devoted to reestablishing law and order.

[10]Professor James Bryce was the author of *The American Commonwealth* (2 volumes, 1888), a classic study of American institutions and society in the nineteenth century.

"See *him!* Great Scott! *No!* If he happens to appear in the office, I have to associate with him; but, thank Heaven, outside of that I move in circles where he cannot come."

And yet the first thing I have been taught to believe is that money was everything in America!

III

"Poor men—God made, and all for that!"

It was a bad business throughout, and the only consolation is that it was all my fault.

A man took me round the Chinese quarter of San Francisco, which is a ward of the city of Canton set down in the most eligible business-quarter of the place.

The Chinaman with his usual skill has possessed himself of good brick fire-proof buildings and, following instinct, has packed each tenement with hundreds of souls, all living in filth and squalor not to be appreciated save by you in India. That cursory investigation ought to have sufficed; but I wanted to know how deep in the earth the Pig-tail had taken root. Therefore I explored the Chinese quarter a second time and alone, which was foolishness. No one in the filthy streets (but for the blessed sea breezes San Francisco would enjoy cholera every season) interfered with movements, though many asked for *cumshaw*. I struck a house about four stories high full of celestial abominations, and began to burrow down; having heard that these tenements were constructed on the lines of icebergs—two-thirds below sight level. Downstairs I crawled past Chinamen in bunks, opium-smokers, brothels, and gambling hells, till I had reached the second cellar—was, in fact, in the labyrinths of a warren. Great is the wisdom of the Chinaman. In time of trouble that house could be razed to the ground by the mob, and yet hide all its inhabitants in brick-walled and wooden-beamed subterranean galleries, strengthened with iron-framed doors and gates. On the second underground floor a man asked for *cumshaw* and took me down-stairs to yet another cellar, where the air was as thick as butter, and the lamps burned little holes in it not more than an inch square. In this place a poker

28

club had assembled and was in full swing. The Chinaman loves "pokel," and plays it with great skill, swearing like a cat when he loses. Most of the men round the table were in semi-European dress, their pig-tails curled up under billycock hats. One of the company looked like a Eurasian, whence I argued that he was a Mexican—a supposition that later inquiries confirmed. They were a picturesque set of fiends and polite, being too absorbed in their game to look at the stranger. We were all deep down under the earth and save for the rustle of a blue gown sleeve and the ghostly whisper of the cards as they were shuffled and played, there was no sound. The heat was almost unendurable. There was some dispute between the Mexican and the man on his left. The latter shifted his place to put the table between himself and his opponent, and stretched a lean yellow hand towards the Mexican's winnings.

Mark how purely man is a creature of instinct. Rarely introduced to the pistol, I saw the Mexican half rise in his chair and at the same instant found myself full length on the floor. None had told me that this was the best attitude when bullets are abroad. I was there prone before I had time to think—dropping as the room filled with an intolerable clamor like the discharge of a cannon. In those close quarters the pistol report had no room to spread any more than the smoke—then acrid in my nostrils. There was no second shot, but a great silence in which I rose slowly to my knees. The Chinaman was gripping the table with both hands and staring in front of him at an empty chair. The Mexican had gone, and a little whirl of smoke was floating near the roof. Still gripping the table, the Chinaman said: "Ah!" in the tone that a man would use when, looking up from his work suddenly, he sees a well-known friend in the doorway. Then he coughed and fell over to his own right, and I saw that he had been shot in the stomach.

I became aware that, save for two men leaning over the stricken one, the room was empty; and all the tides of intense fear, hitherto held back by intenser curiosity, swept over my soul. I ardently desired the outside air. It was possible that the Chinamen would mistake me for the Mexican,—everything horrible seemed possible just then,—and it was more than possible that the stairways would be closed while they were hunting for the murderer. The man on the floor coughed a sickening cough. I heard it as I fled, and one of his companions turned out the lamp. Those stairs seemed interminable, and to add to my dismay there was no sound of commotion in the house. No one hindered, no one even looked at me. There was no trace of the Mexican. I found the doorway and, my legs trembling under me, reached the protection of the clear cool night, the fog, and the rain. I dared not run, and for the life of me I could not walk. I must have effected a compromise, for I remember the light of a street lamp showed the shadow of one half skipping—caracoling along the pavements in what seemed to be an ecstasy of suppressed happiness. But it was fear—deadly fear. Fear compounded of past knowledge of the Oriental —only other white man—available witness—three stories underground—and the cough of the Chinaman now some forty feet under my clattering boot-heels. It was good to see the shop-fronts and electric lights again. Not for anything would I have informed the police, because I firmly believed that the Mexican had been dealt with somewhere down there on the third floor long ere I had reached the air; and, moreover, once clear of the place, I could not for the life of me tell where it was. My ill-considered flight brought me out somewhere a mile distant from the hotel; and the clank of the lift that bore me to a bed six stories above ground was music in my ears. Wherefore I would impress it upon you who follow after, do not knock about the Chinese quarters at night and alone. You may stumble across a picturesque piece of human nature that will unsteady your nerves for half a day.

*

And this brings me by natural sequence to the great drink question. As you know, of course, the American does not drink at meals as a sensible man should. Indeed, he has no meals. He stuffs for ten minutes thrice a day. Also he has no decent notions about the sun being over the yard-arm or below the horizon. He pours his vanity into himself at unholy hours, and indeed he can hardly help it. You have no notion of what "treating" means on the Western slope. It is more than an institution; it is a religion, though men tell me that it is nothing to what it was. Take a very common instance. At 10:30 A.M. a man is smitten with a desire for stimulants. He is in the company of two friends. All three adjourn to the nearest bar,—seldom more than twenty yards away,—and take three straight whiskies. They talk for two minutes. The second and third man then treats in order; and thus each walks into the street, two of them the poorer by three goes of whisky under their belt and one with two more liquors than he wanted. It is not etiquette yet to refuse a treat. The result is peculiar. I have never yet, I confess, seen a drunken man in the streets, but I have heard more about drunkenness among white men, and seen more decent men above or below themselves with drink, than I care to think about. And the vice runs up into all sorts of circles and societies. Never was I more astonished than at one pleasant dinner party to hear a pair of pretty lips say casually of a gentleman friend then under discussion, "He was drunk." The fact was merely stated without emotion. That was what startled me. But the climate of California deals kindly with excess, and treacherously covers up its traces. A man neither bloats nor shrivels in this dry air. He continues with the false bloom of health upon his cheeks, an equable eye, a firm mouth, and a steady hand till a day of reckoning arrives, and suddenly breaking up, about the head, he dies, and his friends speak his epitaph accordingly. Why people who in most cases cannot hold their liquor should play with it so recklessly I leave to others to decide. This unhappy state of affairs has, however, produced one good result which I will confide to you. In the heart of the business quarter, where banks and bankers are thickest, and telegraph wires most numerous, stands a semi-subterranean bar tended by a German with long blond locks and a crystalline eye. Go thither softly treading on the tips of your toes, and ask him for a Button Punch. 'Twill take ten minutes to brew, but the result is the highest and noblest product of the age. No man but one knows what is in it. I have a theory it is compounded of the shavings of cherubs' wings, the glory of a tropical dawn, the red clouds of sunset, and fragments of lost epics by dead masters. But try you for yourselves, and pause a while to bless me, who am always mindful of the truest interests of my brethren.

But enough of the stale spilth of bar-rooms. Turn now to the august spectacle of a Government of the people, by the people, and for the people, as it is understood in the city of San Francisco. Professor Bryce's book will tell you that every American citizen over twenty-one years of age possesses a vote. He may not know how to run his own business, control his wife, or instill reverence into his children, may be pauper, half-crazed with drink, bankrupt, dissolute, or merely a born fool; but he has a vote. If he likes, he can be voting most of his time—voting for his State Governor, his municipal officers, local option, sewage contracts, or anything else of which he has no special knowledge.

Once every four years he votes for a new President. In his spare moments he votes for his own judges—the men who shall give him justice. These are dependent on popular favor for re-election inasmuch as they are but chosen for a term of years—two or three, I believe. Such a position is manifestly best calculated to create an independent and unprejudiced administrator. Now this mass of persons who vote is divided into two parties—Republican and Democrat. They are both agreed in thinking that the other part is running creation (which is America) into red flame. Also the Democrat as a party drinks more than the Republican, and when drunk may be heard to talk about a thing called the Tariff, which he does not understand, but which he conceives to be the bulwark of the country or else the surest power for its destruction. Sometimes he says one thing and sometimes another, in order to contradict the Republican, who is always contradicting himself. And this is a true and lucid account of the forepart of American politics. The behind-part is otherwise.

Since every man has a vote and may vote on every conceivable thing, it follows that there exist certain wise men who understand the art of buying up votes retail, and vending them wholesale to whoever wants them most urgently. Now an American engaged in making a home for himself has not time to vote for turncocks and district attorneys and cattle of that kind, but the unemployed have much time because they are always on hand somewhere in the streets. They are called "the boys," and form a peculiar class. The boys are young men; inexpert in war, unskilled in labor; who neither killed a man, lifted cattle, or dug a well. In plain English, they are just the men in the streets who can always be trusted to rally round any cause that has a glass of liquor for a visible heart. They wait—they are on hand—; and in being on hand lies the crown and glory of American politics. The wise man is he who, keeping a liquor saloon and judiciously dispensing drinks, knows how to retain within arm's reach a block of men who will vote for or against anything under the canopy of heaven. Not every saloonkeeper can do this. It demands careful study of city politics, tact, the power of conciliation, and infinite resources of anecdote to amuse and keep the crowd together night after night, till the saloon becomes a salon. Above all, the liquor side of the scheme must not be worked for immediate profit. The boys who drink so freely will ultimately pay their host a thousandfold. An Irishman, and an Irishman pre-eminently, knows how to work such a saloon parliament. Observe for a moment the plan of operations. The rank and file are treated to drink and a little money—and they vote. He who controls ten votes receives a proportionate reward; the dispenser of a thousand votes is worthy of reverence, and so the chain runs on till we reach the most successful worker of public saloons—the man most skillful in keeping his items together and using them when required. Such a man governs the city as absolutely as a king. And you would know where the gain comes in? The whole of the public offices of a city (with the exception of a very few where special technical skill is required) are short-term offices distributed according to "political" leanings. What would you have? A big city requires many officials. Each office carries a salary and influence worth twice the pay. The offices are for the representatives of the men who keep together and are on hand to vote. The Commissioner of Sewage, let us say, is a gentleman who has been elected to his office by a Republican vote. He knows little and cares less about sewage, but he has sense enough to man the pumping-works and the street-sweeping machines with the gentlemen who elected him. The Commissioner of Police has been helped to his post very largely by the influence of the boys at such and such a saloon. He may be the guardian of city morals, but he is not going to allow his subordinates to enforce early closing or abstention from gambling in that saloon. Most offices are limited to four years, consequently he is a fool who does not make his office pay him while he is in it.

The only people who suffer by this happy arrangement are, in fact, the people who devise the lovely system. And they suffer because they are Americans. Let us explain. As you know, every big city here holds at least one big foreign vote—generally Irish, frequently German. In San Francisco, the gathering place of the races, there is a distinct Italian vote to be considered, but the Irish vote is more important. For this reason the Irishman does not kill himself with overwork. He is made for the cheery dispensing of liquors, for everlasting blarney, and possesses a wonderfully keen appreciation of the weaknesses of lesser human nature. Also he has no sort of conscience, and only one strong conviction—that of deep-rooted hatred toward England. He keeps to the streets, he is on hand, he votes joyously, spending days lavishly, —and time is the American's dearest commodity. Behold the glorious result. To-day the city of San Francisco is governed by the Irish vote and the Irish influence, under the rule of a gentleman whose sight is impaired, and who requires a man to lead him about the streets. He is called officially "Boss Buckley," and unofficially the "Blind White Devil."[1] I have before me now the record of his amiable career in black and white. It occupies four columns of small print, and perhaps you would think it disgraceful. Summarized, it is as follows. Boss Buckley, by tact and deep

[1]Chris Buckley, an Irish immigrant, operated a Bush Street saloon and gambling parlor, which included an exchange dealing in mining stocks. Buckley's eyesight was reported to be so poor that he could not see to read or write. During the 1880s he gained control of the San Francisco City Hall, which enabled him to sell protection to underworld figures; and all who had business, legitimate or otherwise, in the city had to see him first. Buckley controlled enough votes to place his agents in municipal offices and was thus able to award streetcar and railroad franchises and rich public contracts for streets, schools, firehouses, and other projects.

knowledge of the seamy side of the city, won himself a following of voters. He sought no office himself, or rarely: but as his following increased he sold their services to the highest bidder, himself taking toll of the revenues of every office. He controlled the Democratic party in the city of San Francisco. The people appoint their own judges. Boss Buckley's people appointed judges. These judges naturally were Boss Buckley's property. I have been to dinner parties and heard educated men, not concerned with politics, telling stories one to another of "justice," both civil and criminal, being bought with a price from the hands of these judges. Such tales they told without heat, as men recording facts. Contracts for road-mending, public buildings, and the like are under the control of Boss Buckley, because the men whom Buckley's following sent to the City Council adjudicate on these contracts; and on each and every one of these contracts Boss Buckley levies his percentage for himself and his allies.

The Republican party in San Francisco also have their boss. He is not so great a genius as Boss Buckley, but I decline to believe that he is any whit more virtuous. He has a smaller number of votes at his command.

IV

I have been watching machinery in repose after reading about machinery in action.

An excellent gentleman who bears a name honored in the magazines writes, much as Disraeli orated, of "the sublime instincts of an ancient people," the certainty with which they can be trusted to manage their own affairs in their own way, and the speed with which they are making for all sorts of desirable goals. This he called a statement of purview of American politics.

I went almost directly afterwards to a saloon where gentlemen interested in ward politics nightly congregate. They were not pretty persons. Some of them were bloated, and they all swore cheerfully till the heavy gold watch-chains on their fat stomachs rose and fell again; but they talked over their liquor as men who had power and unquestioned access to places of trust and profit.

The magazine-writer discussed theories of government; these men the practice. They had been there. They knew all about it. They banged their fist on the table and spoke of political "pulls," the vending of votes, and so forth. Theirs was not the talk of village babblers reconstructing the affairs of the nation, but of strong, coarse, lustful men fighting for spoil and thoroughly understanding the best methods of reaching it. I listened long and intently to speech I could not understand, or only in spots. It was the speech of business, however. I had sense enough to know *that,* and to do my laughing outside the door. Then I began to understand why my pleasant and well-educated hosts in San Francisco spoke with bitter scorn of such duties of citizenship as voting and taking an interest in the distribution of offices. Scores of men have told me with no false pride that they would as soon concern themselves with the public affairs of the City or State as rake muck. Read about politics as the cultured writer of the magazines regards 'em, and then, *and not till then,* pay your respects to the gentlemen who run the grimy reality.

I'm sick of interviewing night-editors, who, in response to my demand for the record of a prominent citizen, answer: "Well, you see, he began by keeping a saloon," etc. I prefer to believe that my informants are treating me as in the old sinful days in India I was used to treat our wandering Globe-trotters. They declare that they speak the truth, and the news of dog-politics lately vouchsafed to me in groggeries incline me to believe—but I won't. The people are much too nice to slangander as recklessly as I have been doing. Besides, I am hopelessly in love with about eight American maidens—all perfectly delightful till the next one comes into the room. O-Toyo was a darling, but she lacked several things; conversation, for one. You cannot live on giggles. She shall remain unmoved at Nagasaki while I roast a battered heart before the shrine of a big Kentucky blonde who had for a nurse, when she was little, a negro "mammy." By consequence she was welded on to California beauty, Paris dresses, Eastern culture, Europe trips, and wild Western originality, the queer dreamy superstitions of the negro quarters, and the result is soul-shattering. And she is but one of many stars. *Item,* a maiden who believes in education and possesses it, with a few hundred thousand dollars to boot, and a taste for slumming. *Item,* the leader of a sort of informal salon where girls congregate, read papers, and daringly discuss metaphysical problems and candy—a sloe-eyed, black-browed imperious maiden. *Item,* a very small maiden, absolutely without reverence, who can in one swift sentence trample upon and leave gasping half a dozen young men. *Item,* a millionairess, burdened with her money, lonely, caustic, with a tongue keen as a sword, yearning for a sphere, but chained up to the rock of her vast possessions. *Item,* a typewriter-maiden earning her own bread in this big city, because she doesn't think a girl ought to be a burden on her parents. She quotes Théophile Gautier, and moves through the world manfully, much respected, for all her twenty inexperienced summers. *Item,* a woman from Cloudland who has no history in the past, but is discreetly of the present, and strives for the confidences of male humanity on the grounds of "sympathy." (This is not altogether a new type.) *Item,* a girl in a "dive" blessed with a Greek head and eyes that seem to speak all that is best and sweetest in the world. But woe is me!—she has no ideas in this world or the next, beyond the consumption of beer (a commission on each bottle), and protests that she sings the songs allotted to her nightly with no more than the vaguest notion of their meaning.

Sweet and comely are the maidens of Devonshire; delicate and of gracious seeming those who live in the pleasant places of London; fascinating for all their demureness the damsels of France clinging closely to their mothers, and with large eyes wondering at the wicked world; excellent in her own place and to those who understand her is the Anglo-Indian "spin" in her second season; but the girls of America are above and beyond them all. They are clever; they can talk. Yea, it is said that they think. Certainly they have an appearance of so doing. They are original, and look you between the brows with unabashed eyes as a sister might look at her brother. They are instructed in the folly and vanity of the male mind, for they have associated with "the boys" from babyhood, and can discerningly minister to both vices, or pleasantly snub the possessor. They possess, moreover, a life among themselves, independent of masculine associations. They have societies and clubs and unlimited tea-fights where all the guests are girls. They are self-possessed without parting with any tenderness that is their sex-right; they understand; they can take care of themselves; they are superbly independent. When you ask them what makes them so charming, they say: "It is because we are better educated than your girls and—and we are more sensible in regard to men. We have good times all around, but we aren't taught to regard every man as a possible husband. Nor is he expected to marry the first girl he calls on regularly." Yes, they have good times, their freedom is large, and they do not abuse it. They can go driving with young men, and receive visits from young men to an extent that would make an English mother wink with horror; and neither driver nor drivee have a thought beyond the enjoyment of a good time. As certain also of their own poets have said:—

> "Man is fire and woman is tow,
> And the devil he comes and begins to blow."

In America the tow is soaked in a solution that makes it fireproof, in absolute liberty and large knowledge: consequently accidents do not exceed the regular percentage arranged by the Devil for each class and climate under the skies. But the freedom of the young girl has its drawbacks. She is—I say it with all reluctance— irreverent, from her forty-dollar bonnet to the buckles in her eighteen-dollar shoes. She talks flippantly to her parents and men old enough to be her grandfather. She has a prescriptive right to the society of the Man who Arrives. The parents admit it. This is sometimes embarrassing, especially when you call on a man and his wife for the sake of information; the one being a merchant of varied knowledge, the other a woman of the world. In five minutes your host has vanished. In another five his wife has followed him, and you are left with a very charming maiden doubtless, but certainly not the person you came to see. She chatters and you grin; but you leave with the very strong impression of a wasted morning. This has been my experience once or twice. I have even said as pointedly as I dared to a man: "I came to see you." "You'd better see me in my office, then. The house belongs to my womenfolk—to my daughter, that is to say." He spoke with truth. The American of wealth is owned by his family. They exploit him for bullion, and sometimes it seems to me that his lot is a lonely one. The women get the ha'pence; the kicks are all his own. Nothing is too good for an American's daughter (I speak here of the moneyed classes). The girls take every gift as a matter of course. Yet they develop greatly when a catastrophe arrives and the man of many millions goes up or goes down and his daughters take to stenography or typewriting. I have heard many tales of heroism from the lips of girls who counted the principals among their friends. The crash came; Mammie or Hattie or Sadie gave up their maid, their carriages and candy, and with a No. 2 Remington and a stout heart set about earning their daily bread.

"And did I drop her from the list of my friends? No, sir," said a scarlet-lipped vision in white lace. "That might happen to me any day."

It may be this sense of possible disaster in the air that makes

San Franciscan society go with so captivating a rush and whirl. Recklessness is in the air. I can't explain where it comes from, but there it is. The roaring winds off the Pacific make you drunk to begin with. The aggressive luxury on all sides helps out the intoxication, and you spin for ever "down the ringing groves of change" (there is no small change, by the way, west of the Rockies) as long as money lasts. They make greatly and they spend lavishly; not only the rich but the artisans, who pay nearly five pounds for a suit of clothes and for other luxuries in proportion. The young men rejoice in the days of their youth. They gamble, yacht, race, enjoy prizefights and cock-fights—the one openly, the other in secret—they establish luxurious clubs; they break themselves over horseflesh and—other things; and they are instant in quarrel. At twenty they are experienced in business; embark in vast enterprises, take partners as experienced as themselves, and go to pieces with as much splendor as their neighbors. Remember that the men who stocked California in the Fifties were physically, and as far as regards certain tough virtues, the pick of the earth. The inept and the weakly died *en route* or went under in the days of construction. To this nucleus were added all the races of the Continent—French, Italian, German, and, of course, the Jew. The result you shall see in large-boned, deep-chested, delicate-handed women, and long, elastic, well-built boys. It needs no little golden badge swinging from his watch-chain to mark the Native Son of the Golden West—the country-bred of California. Him I love because he is devoid of fear, carries himself like a man, and has a heart as big as his boots. I fancy, too, he knows how to enjoy the blessings of life that his world so abundantly bestows upon him. At least I heard a little rat of a creature with hock-bottle shoulders explaining that a man from Chicago could pull the eye-teeth of a Californian in business. Well, if I lived in Fairyland, where cherries were as big as plums, plums as big as apples, and strawberries of no account; where the procession of the fruits of the seasons was like a pageant in a Drury Lane pantomime and where the dry air was wine, I should let business slide once in a way and kick up my heels with my fellows. The tale of the resources of California—

vegetable and mineral—is a fairy tale. You can read it in books. You would never believe me. All manner of nourishing food from sea-fish to beef may be bought at the lowest prices; and the people are well developed and of a high stomach. They demand ten shillings for tinkering a jammed lock of a trunk; they receive sixteen shillings a day for working as carpenters; they spend many sixpences on very bad cigars, and they go mad over a prize-fight. When they disagree, they do so fatally, with firearms in their hands, and on the public streets. I was just clear of Mission Street when the trouble began between two gentlemen, one of whom perforated the other. When a policeman, whose name I do not recollect, "fatally shot Ed. Kearney," for attempting to escape arrest, I was in the next street. For these things I am thankful. It is enough to travel with a policeman in a tram-car and while he arranges his coat-tails as he sits down, to catch sight of a loaded revolver. It is enough to know that fifty per cent. of the men in the public saloons carry pistols about them. The Chinaman waylays his adversary and methodically chops him to pieces with his hatchet. Then the Press roar about the brutal ferocity of the Pagan. The Italian reconstructs his friend with a long knife. The Press complains of the waywardness of the alien. The Irishman and the native Californian in their hours of discontent use the revolver, not once, but six times. The Press records the fact, and asks in the next column whether the world can parallel the progress of San Francisco. The American who loves his country will tell you that this sort of thing is confined to the lower classes. Just at present an ex-judge who was sent to jail by another judge (upon my word, I cannot tell whether these titles mean anything) is breathing red-hot vengeance against his enemy. The papers have interviewed both parties and confidently expect a fatal issue.

Now let me draw breath and curse the negro waiter and through him the negro in service generally. He has been made a citizen with a vote; consequently both political parties play with him. But that is neither here nor there. He will commit in one meal every *bétise* that a scullion fresh from the plowtail is capable of, and he will continue to repeat those faults. He is as complete a heavy-footed uncomprehending, bungle-fisted fool as any *mem-*

sahib in the East ever took into her establishment. But he is according to law a free and independent citizen—consequently above reproof or criticism. He, and he alone, in this insane city will wait at table (the Chinaman doesn't count). He is untrained, inept, but he will fill the place and draw the pay. Now God and his father's Kismet made him intellectually inferior to the Oriental. He insists on pretending that he serves tables by accident—as a sort of amusement. He wishes you to understand this little fact. You wish to eat your meals, and if possible to have them properly served. He is a big, black, vain baby and a man rolled into one. A colored gentleman who insisted on getting me pie when I wanted something else, demanded information about India. I gave him some facts about wages. "Oh hell," said he, cheerfully, "that wouldn't keep me in cigars for a month." Then he fawned on me for a ten-cent piece. Later he took it upon himself to pity the natives of India—"heathen" he called them, this Woolly One whose race has been the butt of every comedy on the Asiatic stage since the beginning. And I turned and saw by the head upon his shoulders that he was a Yoruba man, if there be any truth in ethnological castes. He did his thinking in English, but he was a Yoruba negro, and the race type had remained the same throughout his generations. And the room was full of other races—some that looked exactly like Gallas (but the trade was never recruited from that side of Africa), some duplicates of Cameroon heads, and some Kroomen, if ever Kroomen wore evening dress. The American does not consider little matters of descent, though by this time he ought to know all about "damnable heredity." As a general rule he keeps himself very far from the negro and says unpretty things about him. There are six million negroes more or less in the States, and they are increasing. The Americans once having made them citizens cannot unmake them. He says, in his newspapers, they ought to be elevated by education. He is trying this: but it is like to be a long job, because black blood is much more adhesive than white, and throws back with annoying persistence. When the negro gets a religion he returns directly as a hiving bee, to the first instincts of his people. Just now a wave of religion is sweeping over some of the Southern

States. Up to the present, two Messiahs and one Daniel have appeared; and several human sacrifices have been offered up to these incarnations. The Daniel managed to get three young men, who he insisted were Shadrach, Meshach, and Abednego, to walk into a blast furnace; guaranteeing non-combustion. They did not return. I have seen nothing of this kind, but I have attended a negro church. The congregation were moved by the spirit to groans and tears, and one of them danced up the aisle to the mourners' bench. The motive may have been genuine. The movements of the shaken body were those of a Zanzibar stick-dance, such as you see at Aden on the coal boats; and even as I watched the people, the links that bound them to the white man snapped one by one, and I saw before me—the *hubshi* (the Woolly One) praying to the God he did not understand. Those neatly dressed folk on the benches, the gray-headed elder by the window, were savages—neither more nor less. What will the American do with the Negro? The South will not consort with him. In some States miscegenation is a penal offense. The North is every year less and less in need of his services. And he will not disappear. He will continue as a problem. His friends will urge that he is as good as the white man. His enemies . . . it is not good to be a negro in the land of the free and the home of the brave.

But this has nothing to do with San Francisco and her merry maidens, her strong, swaggering men, and her wealth of gold and pride. They bore me to a banquet in honor of a brave Lieutenant—Carlin, of the *Vandalia*—who stuck by his ship in the great cyclone at Apia and comported himself as an officer should. On that occasion—'twas at the Bohemian Club—I heard oratory with the roundest of *o*'s; and devoured a dinner the memory of which will descend with me into the hungry grave. There were about forty speeches delivered; and not one of them was average or ordinary. It was my first introduction to the American Eagle screaming for all it was worth. The Lieutenant's heroism served as a peg from which those silver-tongued ones turned themselves loose and kicked. They ransacked the clouds of sunset, the thunderbolts of Heaven, the deeps of Hell, and the splendors of the Resurrection, for tropes and metaphors, and hurled the result at the head of the guest of the evening. Never since the morning stars sang together for joy, I learned, had an amazed creation witnessed such superhuman bravery as that displayed by the American navy in the Samoa cyclone. Till earth rotted in the phosphorescent star-and-stripe slime of a decayed universe that Godlike gallantry would not be forgotten. I grieve that I cannot give the exact words. My attempt at reproducing their spirit is pale and inadequate. I sat bewildered on a coruscating Niagara of—blatherumskite. It was magnificent—it was stupendous; and I was conscious of a wicked desire to hide my face in a napkin and grin. Then, according to rule, they produced their dead, and across the snowy tablecloths dragged the corpse of every man slain in the Civil War, and hurled defiance at "our natural enemy" (England, so please you!) "with her chain of fortresses across the world." Thereafter they glorified their nation afresh, from the beginning, in case any detail should have been overlooked, and that made me uncomfortable for their sakes. How in the world can a white man, a Sahib of Our blood, stand up and plaster praise on his own country? He can think as highly as he likes, but his open-mouthed vehemence of adoration struck me almost as indelicate. My hosts talked for rather more than three hours, and at the end seemed ready for three hours more. But when the Lieutenant—such a big, brave, gentle giant!—rose to his feet, he delivered what seemed to me as the speech of the evening. I remember nearly the whole of it, and it ran something in this way: "Gentlemen—it's very good of you to give me this dinner and to tell me all these pretty things, but what I want you to understand—that fact is—what we want and what we ought to get at once is a navy—more ships—lots of 'em—" Then we howled the top of the roof off, and I, for one, fell in love with Carlin on the spot. Wallah! He was a man.

The Prince among merchants bade me take no heed to the warlike sentiments of some of the old Generals. "The sky-rockets are thrown in for effect," quoth he, "and whenever we get on our hind legs we always express a desire to chaw up England. It's a sort of family affair."

And indeed, when you come to think of it, there is no other country for the American public speaker to trample upon.

France has Germany; we have Russia; for Italy, Austria is provided; and the humblest Pathan possesses an ancestral enemy. Only America stands out of the racket; and therefore to be in fashion, makes a sand-bag of the mother-country, and bangs her when occasion requires. "The chain of fortresses" man, a fascinating talker, explained to me after the affair that he was compelled to blow off steam. Everybody expected it. When we had chanted "The Star-Spangled Banner" not more than eight times, we adjourned. America is a very great country, but it is not yet Heaven with electric lights and plush fittings, as the speakers professed to believe. My listening mind went back to the politicians in the saloon who wasted no time in talking about freedom, but quietly made arrangements to impose their will on the citizens. "The Judge is a great man, but give thy presents to the Clerk," as the proverb saith.

And what more remains to tell? I cannot write connectedly, because I am in love with all those girls aforesaid and some others who do not appear in the invoice. The type-writer girl is an institution of which the comic papers make much capital, but she is vastly convenient. She and a companion rent a room in a business quarter, and copy manuscript at the rate of six annas a page. Only a woman can manage a type-writing machine, because she has served apprenticeship to the sewing-machine. She can earn as much as a hundred dollars a month, and professes to regard this form of bread-winning as her natural destiny. But oh how she hates it in her heart of hearts! When I had got over the surprise of doing business and trying to give orders to a young woman of coldly clerkly aspect, intrenched behind gold-rimmed spectacles, I made inquiries concerning the pleasures of this independence. They liked it—indeed, they did. 'Twas the natural fate of almost all girls,—the recognized custom in America,—and I was a barbarian not to see it in that light.

"Well, and after?" said I. "What happens?"

"We work for our bread."

"And then what do you expect?"

"Then we shall work for our bread."

"Till you die?"

"Ye-es—unless——"

"Unless what? A man works till he dies."

"So shall we." This without enthusiasm—"I suppose."

Said the partner in the firm audaciously: "Sometimes we marry our employers—at least that's what the newspapers say." The hand banged on half a dozen of the keys of the machine at once. "Yes, I don't care. I hate it—I hate it—I *hate* it, and you needn't look so!"

The senior partner was regarding the rebel with grave-eyed reproach.

"I thought you did," said I. "I don't suppose American girls are much different from English ones in instinct."

"Isn't it Théophile Gautier who says that the only differences between country and country lie in the slang and the uniform of the police?"

Now in the name of all the Gods at once, what is one to say to a young lady (who in England would be a Person) who earns her own bread and very naturally hates the employ, and slings out-of-the-way quotations at your head? That one falls in love with her goes without saying; but that is not enough.

A mission should be established.

V

"I walked in the lonesome even,
    And who so sad as I,
As I saw the young men and maidens
    Merrily passing by?"

San Francisco has only one drawback. 'Tis hard to leave. When
like the pious Hans Breitmann I "cut that city by the sea" it was
with regrets for the pleasant places left behind, for the men who
were so clever, and the women who were so witty, for the "dives,"
the beer-halls, the bucket-shops, and the poker-hells where humanity was going to the Devil with shouting and laughter and
song and the rattle of dice-boxes.[1] I would fain have stayed, but
I feared that an evil end would come to me when my money was
all spent and I descended to the street corner. A voice inside me
said: "Get out of this. Go north. Strike for Victoria and Vancouver. Bask for a day under the shadow of the old flag." So I
set forth from San Francisco to Portland in Oregon, and that was
a railroad run of thirty-six hours.

The Oakland railway terminus, whence all the main lines start,
does not own anything approaching to a platform. A yard with a
dozen or more tracks is roughly asphalted, and the traveler laden
with handbags skips merrily across the metals in search of his own
particular train. The bells of half a dozen shunting engines are
tolling suggestively in his ears. If he is run down, so much the
worse for him. "When the bell rings, look out for the locomotive."
Long use has made the nation familiar and even contemptuous
towards trains to an extent which God never intended. Women

[1] Hans Breitman was the pseudonym of Charles Godfrey Leland, American author, editor, philologist, and educator. During the 1880s he introduced industrial and craft arts into American schools.

47

who in England would gather up their skirts and scud timorously over a level crossing in the country, here talk dress and babies under the very nose of the cow-catcher, and little children dally with the moving car in a manner horrible to behold. We pulled out at the wholly insignificant speed of twenty-five miles an hour through the streets of a suburb of fifty thousand, and in our progress among the carts and the children and shop fronts slew nobody; at which I was not a little disappointed.

When the negro porter bedded me up for the night and I had solved the problem of undressing while lying down,—I was much cheered by the thought that if anything happened I should have to stay where I was and wait till the kerosene lamps set the overturned car alight and burned me to death. It is easier to get out of a full theater than to leave a Pullman in haste.

By the time I had discovered that a profusion of nickel-plating, plush, and damask does not compensate for closeness and dust, the train ran into the daylight on the banks of the Sacramento River. A few windows were gingerly opened after the bunks had been reconverted into seats, but that long coffin-car was by no means ventilated, and we were a gummy, grimy crew who sat there. At six in the morning the heat was distinctly unpleasant, but seeing with the eye of the flesh that I was in Bret Harte's own country, I rejoiced. There were the pines and madrone-clad hills his miners lived and fought among; there was the heated red earth that showed whence the gold had been washed; the dry gulch, the red, dusty road where Hamblin was used to stop the stage in the intervals of his elegant leisure and superior card-play; there was the timber felled and sweating resin in the sunshine; and, above all, there was the quivering pungent heat that Bret Harte drives into your dull brain with the magic of his pen. When we stopped at a collection of packing-cases dignified by the name of a town, my felicity was complete. The name of the place was something offensive,—Amberville or Jacksonburg,—but it owned a cast-iron fountain worthy of a town of thirty thousand. Next to the fountain was a "hotel," at least seventeen feet high including the chimney, and next to the hotel was the forest—the pine, the oak, and the untrammelled undergrowth of the hillside. A cinnamon-bear cub—

Baby Sylvester in the very fur—was tied to the stump of a tree opposite the fountain; a pack-mule dozed in the dust-haze, a red-shirted miner in a slouch hat supported the hotel, a blue-shirted miner swung round the corner, and the two went indoors for a drink. A girl came out of the only other house but one, and shading her eyes with a brown hand stared at the panting train. She didn't recognize me, but I knew her—had known her for years. She was M'liss. She never married the schoolmaster, after all, but stayed, always young and always fair, among the pines. I knew Red-shirt too. He was one of the bearded men who stood back when Tennessee claimed his partner from the hands of the Law. The Sacramento River, a few yards away, shouted that all these things were true. The train went on while Baby Sylvester stood on his downy head, and M'liss swung her sun-bonnet by the strings.

"What do you think?" said a lawyer who was traveling with me. "It's a new world to you; isn't it?"

"No. It's quite familiar. I was never out of England; it's as if I saw it all."

Quick as light came the answer: "'Yes, they lived once thus at Venice when the miners were the kings.'"

I loved that lawyer on the spot. We drank to Bret Harte who, you remember, "claimed California, but California never claimed him. He's turned English."

Lying back in state, I waited for the flying miles to turn over the pages of the book I knew. They brought me all I desired—from Man of no Account sitting on a stump and playing with a dog, to "that most sarcastic man, the quiet Mister Brown." He boarded the train from out of the woods, and there was venom and sulphur on his tongue. He had just lost a lawsuit. Only Yuba Bill failed to appear. The train had taken his employment from him. A nameless ruffian backed me into a corner and began telling me about the resources of the country, and what it would eventually become. All I remember of his lecture was that you could catch trout in the Sacramento River—the stream that we followed so faithfully.

Then rose a tough and wiry old man with grizzled hair and made inquiries about the trout. To him was added the secretary of a life-insurance company. I fancy he was traveling to rake in the dead that the train killed. But he, too, was a fisherman, and the two turned to meward. The frankness of a Westerner is delightful. They tell me that in the Eastern States I shall meet another type of man and a more reserved. The Californian always speaks of the man from the New England States as a different breed. It is our Punjab and Madras over again, but more so. The old man was on a holiday in search of fish. When he discovered a brother-loafer he proposed a confederation of rods. Quoth the insurance-agent, "I'm not staying any time in Portland, but I will introduce you to a man there who'll tell you about fishing." The two told strange tales as we slid through the forests and saw afar off the snowy head of a great mountain. There were vineyards, fruit orchards, and wheat fields where the land opened out, and every ten miles or so, twenty or thirty wooden houses and at least three churches. A large town would have a population of two thousand and an infinite belief in its own capacities. Sometimes a flaring advertisement flanked the line, calling for men to settle down, take up the ground, and make their home there. At a big town we could pick up the local newspaper, narrow as the cutting edge of a chisel and twice as keen—a journal filled with the prices of stock, notices of improved reaping and binding machines, movements of eminent citizens—"whose fame beyond their own abode extends—for miles along the Harlem road." There was not much grace about these papers, but all breathed the same need for good men, steady men who would plow, and till, and build schools for their children, and make a township in the hills. Once only I found a sharp change in the note and a very pathetic one. I think it was a young soul in trouble who was writing poetry. The editor had jammed the verses between the flamboyant advertisement of a real-estate agent—a man who sells you land and lies about it—and that of a Jew tailor who disposed of "nobby" suits at "cut-throat prices." Here are two verses; I think they tell their own story:—

> "God made the pine with its root in the earth,
>   Its top in the sky;
> They have burned the pine to increase the worth

Of the wheat and the silver rye.
"Go weigh the cost of the soul of the pine
    Cut off from the sky;
And the price of the wheat that grows so fine
    And the worth of the silver rye!"

The thin-lipped, keen-eyed men who boarded the train would not read that poetry, or, if they did, would not understand. Heaven guard that poor pine in the desert and keep "its top in the sky!"

When the train took to itself an extra engine and began to breathe heavily, some one said that we were ascending the Siskiyou Mountains. We had been climbing steadily from San Francisco, and at last won to over four thousand feet above sea-level, always running through forest. Then, naturally enough, we came down, but we dropped two thousand two hundred feet in about thirteen miles. It was not so much the grinding of the brakes along the train, or the sight of three curves of track apparently miles below us, or even the vision of a goods-train apparently just under our wheels, or even the tunnels, that made me reflect; it was the trestles over which we crawled,—trestles something over a hundred feet high and looking like a collection of match-sticks.

"I guess our timber is as much a curse as a blessing," said the old man from Southern California. "These trestles last very well for five or six years; then they get out of repair, and a train goes through 'em, or else a forest fire burns 'em up."

This was said in the middle of a groaning, shivering trestle. An occasional plate-layer took a look at us as we went down, but that railway didn't waste men on inspection duty. Very often there were cattle on the track, against which the engine used a diabolical form of whistling. The old man had been a driver in his youth, and beguiled the way with cheery anecdotes of what might be expected if we fouled a young calf.

"You see, they get their legs under the cow-catcher, and that'll put an engine off the line. I remember when a hog wrecked an excursion-train and killed sixty people. 'Guess the engineer will look out, though."

There is considerably too much guessing about this large nation. As one of them put it rather forcibly: "We guess a trestle will stand forever and we guess that we can patch up a washout on the track, and we guess the road's clear, and sometimes we guess ourselves into the depot, and sometimes we guess ourselves into Hell."

*

The descent brought us far into Oregon and a timber and wheat country. We drove through wheat and pine in alternate slices, but pine chiefly, till we reached Portland, which is a city of fifty thousand, possessing the electric light of course, equally, of course, devoid of pavements, and a port of entry about a hundred miles from the sea at which big steamers can load. It is a poor city that cannot say it has no equal on the Pacific coast. Portland shouts this to the pines which run down from a thousand-foot ridge clear up to the city. You may sit in a bedizened bar-room furnished with with telephone and clicker, and in half an hour be in the woods.

Portland produces lumber and jig-saw fittings for houses, and beer and buggies, and bricks and biscuit; and, in case you should miss the fact, there are glorified views of the town hung up in public places with the value of the products set down in dollars. All this is excellent and exactly suitable to the opening of a new country; but when a man tells you it is civilization, you object. The first thing that the civilized man learns to do is to keep the dollars in the background, because they are only the oil of the machine that makes life go smoothly.

Portland is so busy that it can't attend to its own sewage or paving, and the four-story brick blocks front cobble-stones and plank sidewalks and other things much worse. I saw a foundation being dug out. The sewage of perhaps twenty years ago, had thoroughly soaked into the soil, and there was a familiar and Oriental look about the compost that flew up with each shovel-load. Yet the local papers, as was just and proper, swore there was no place like Portland, Oregon, U.S.A., chronicled the performances of Oregonians, "claimed" prominent citizens elsewhere as Oregonians, and fought tooth and nail for dock, rail, and wharfage projects. And you could find men who had thrown in their lives with the city who were bound up in it, and worked their life out for what they conceived to be its material prosperity. Pity it is to record that in this strenuous, laboring town there had been, a week before, a shooting-case. One well-known man had shot another on the street, and was now pleading self-defence, because the other man had, or the murderer thought he had, a pistol about him. Not content with shooting him dead, he squibbed off his revolver into him as he lay. I read the pleadings, and they made me ill. So far as I could judge, if the dead man's body had been found with a pistol on it, the shooter would have gone free. Apart from the mere murder, cowardly enough in itself, there was a re-finement of cowardice in the plea. Here in this civilized city the surviving brute was afraid he would be shot—fancied he saw the other man make a motion to his hip-pocket, and so on. Eventually the jury disagreed. And the degrading thing was that the trial was reported by men who evidently understood all about the pistol, was tried before a jury who were versed in the etiquette of the hip-pocket, and was discussed on the streets by men equally initiate.

But let us return to more cheerful things. The insurance-agent introduced us as friends to a real-estate man, who promptly bade us go up the Columbia River for a day while he made inquiries about fishing. There was no overwhelming formality. The old man was addressed as "California," I answered indifferently to "England" or "Johnny Bull," and the real-estate man was "Port-land." This was a lofty and spacious form of address.

So California and I took a steamboat, and upon a sumptuous blue and gold morning steered up the Willamette River, on which Portland stands, into the great Columbia—the river that brings the salmon that goes into the tin that is emptied into the dish when the extra guest arrives in India. California introduced me to the boat and the scenery, showed me the "texas," the difference between a "tow-head" and a "sawyer," and the precise nature of a "slue." All I remember is a delightful feeling that Mark Twain's Huckleberry Finn and Mississippi Pilot were quite true, and that I could almost recognize the very reaches down which Huck and Jim had drifted. We were on the border line between Oregon State and Washington Territory, but that didn't matter.[2] The Columbia was the Mississippi so far as I was concerned. We ran along the sides of wooded islands whose banks were caving in with perpetual smashes, and we skipped from one side to another of the mile-wide stream in search of a channel, exactly like a Mississippi steamer, and when we wanted to pick up or set down a passenger we chose a soft and safe place on the shore and ran our very snub nose against it. California spoke to each new passenger as he came aboard and told me the man's birthplace. A long-haired tender of kine crushed out of the underwood, waved his hat, and was taken aboard forthwith. "South Carolina," said California, almost without looking at him. "When he talks you will hear a softer dialect than mine." And it befell as he said: whereat I marveled, and California chuckled. Every island in the river carried fields of rich wheat, orchards, and a white, wooden-house; or else, if the pines grew very thickly, a sawmill, the tremulous whine of whose saws flickered across the water like the drone of a tired bee. From remarks he let fall I gathered that California owned timber ships and dealt in lumber, had ranches too, a partner, and everything handsome about him; in addition to a checkered career of some thirty-five years. But he looked almost as disreputable a loafer as I.

"Say, young feller, we're going to see scenery now. You shout and sing," said California, when the bland wooded islands gave place to bolder outlines, and the steamer ran herself into a hornet's nest of black-fanged rocks not a foot below the boiling broken water. We were trying to get up a slue, or back channel, by a short cut, and the stern-wheel never spun twice in the same direction. Then we hit a floating log with a jar that ran through our system, and then, white-bellied, open-gilled, spun by a dead salmon—a lordly twenty pound Chinook salmon who had perished in his pride. "You'll see the salmon-wheels 'fore long," said a man who lived "way back on the Washoogle," and whose hat was spangled with trout-flies. "Those Chinook salmon never rise to fly. The canneries take them by the wheel." At the next bend we sighted a wheel—an infernal arrangement of wire-gauze compart-

[2]Washington Territory was admitted to the Union, November 11, 1889.

ments worked by the current and moved out from a barge in shore to scoop up the salmon as he races up the river. California swore long and fluently at the sight, and the more fluently when he was told of the weight of a good night's catch—some thousands of pounds. Think of the black and bloody murder of it! But you out yonder insist on buying tinned salmon, and the canneries cannot live by letting down lines.

About this time California was struck with madness. I found him dancing on the fore-deck shouting, "Isn't she a daisy? Isn't she a darling? He had found a waterfall—a blown thread of white vapor that broke from the crest of a hill—a waterfall eight hundred and fifty feet high whose voice was even louder than the voice of the river. "Bridal Veil," jerked out the purser. "D—n that purser and the people who christened her! Why didn't they call her Mechlin lace Falls at fifty dollars a yard while they were at it?" said California. And I agreed with him. There are many "bridal veil" falls in this country, but few, men say, lovelier than those that come down to the Columbia River. Then the scenery began—poured forth with the reckless profusion of Nature, who when she wants to be amiable succeeds only in being oppressively magnificent. The river was penned between gigantic stone walls crowned with the ruined bastions of Oriental palaces. The stretch of green water widened and was guarded by pine-clad hills three thousand feet high. A wicked devil's thumb nail of rock shot up a hundred feet in midstream. A sand-bar of blinding white sand gave promise of flat country that the next bend denied; for, lo! we were running under a triple tier of fortification, lava-topped, pine-clothed, and terrible. Behind them the white dome of Mount Hood ran fourteen thousand feet into the blue, and at their feet the river threshed among a belt of cottonwood trees. There I sat down and looked at California half out of the boat in his anxiety to see both sides of the river at once. He had seen my note-book, and it offended him. "Young feller, let her go—and you shut your head. It's not you nor anybody like you can put this down. Black, the novelist, he could. He can describe salmon-fishing, *he* can." And he flared at me as though he expected me to go on and do likewise.

"I can't. I know it," I said humbly.

"Then thank God that you came along this way."

We reached a little railway, on an island, which was to convey us to a second steamer, because, as the purser explained, the river was a "trifle broken." We had a six-mile run, sitting in the sunshine on a dummy-wagon, whirled just along the edge of the river-bluffs. Sometimes we dived into the fragrant pine woods, ablaze with flowers; but we generally watched the river now narrowed into a turbulent millrace. Just where the whole body of water broke in riot over a series of cascades, the United States Government had chosen to build a lock for steamers, and the stream was one boiling, spouting mob of water. A log shot down the race, struck on a rock, split from end to end, and rolled over in white foam. I shuddered because my toes were not more than sixty feet above the log, and I feared that a stray splinter might have found me. But the train ran into the river on a sort of floating trestle, and I was upon another steamer ere I fully understood why. The cascades were not two hundred yards below us, and when we cast off to go upstream, the rush of the river, ere the wheel struck the water, dragged us as though we had been towed. Then the country opened out, and California mourned for his lost bluffs and crags, till we struck a rock wall four hundred feet high, crowned by the gigantic figure of a man watching us. On a rocky island we saw the white tomb of an old-time settler who had made his money in San Francisco, but who had chosen to be buried in an Indian burying-ground. A decayed wooden "wickyup," where the bones of the Indian dead are laid, almost touched the tomb. The river ran into a canal of basaltic rock, painted in yellow, vermilion, and green by Indians and, by inferior brutes, adorned with advertisements of "bile beans." We had reached The Dalles—the center of a great sheep and wool district, and the head of navigation.

When an American arrives at a new town it is his bounded duty to "take it in." California swung his coat over his shoulder with the gesture of a man used to long tramps, and together, at eight in the evening, we explored The Dalles. The sun had not yet set, and it would be light for at least another hour. All the inhabitants seemed to own a little villa and one church apiece. The young men were out walking with the young maidens, the old folks were sitting on the front steps,—not the ones that led to the religiously shuttered best drawing-room, but the side-front steps, and the husbands and wives were tying back pear trees or gathering cherries. A scent of hay reached me, and in the stillness we could hear the cattle bells as the cows came home across the lava-sprinkled fields. California swung down the wooden pavements, audibly criticising the housewives' hollyhocks and the more perfect ways of pear-grafting, and, as the young men and maidens passed, giving quaint stories of his youth. I felt that I knew all the people aforetime, I was so interested in them and their life. A woman hung over a gate talking to another woman, and as I passed I heard her say, "skirts," and again "skirts," and "I'll send you over the pattern;" and I knew they were talking dress. We stumbled upon a young couple saying good-by in the twilight, and "When shall I see you again?" quoth he; and I understood that to the doubting heart the tiny little town we paraded in twenty minutes might be as large as all London and as impassable as an armed camp. I gave them both my blessing, because "When shall I see you again?" is a question that lies very near to hearts of all the world. The last garden gate shut with a click that traveled far down the street, and the lights of the comfortable families began to shine in the confidingly un-curtained windows.

"Say, Johnny Bull, doesn't all this make you feel lonesome?" said California. "Have you got any folks at home? So've I—a wife and five children—and I'm only on a holiday."

"And I'm only on a holiday," I said, and we went back to the Spittoon-wood Hotel. Alas! for the peace and purity of the little town that I had babbled about. At the back of a shop, and dis-creetly curtained, was a room where the young men who had been talking to the young maidens could play poker and drink and swear, and in the shop were dime novels of bloodshed to corrupt the mind of the little boy, and prurient servant-girl-slush yarns to poison the mind of the girl. California only laughed grimly. He said that all these little one-house towns were pretty much the same all over the States.

That night I dreamed I was back in India with no place to sleep in; tramping up and down the Station mall and asking everybody, "When shall I see you again?"

VI

"The race is neither to the swift
nor the battle to the strong;
but time and chance cometh to all."

I have lived!

The American Continent may now sink under the sea, for I have taken the best that it yields, and the best was neither dollars, love, nor real estate.

Hear now, gentlemen of the Punjab Fishing Club, who whip the reaches of the Tavi, and you who painfully import trout to Ootacamund, and I will tell you how "old man California" and I went fishing, and you shall envy.

We returned from The Dalles to Portland by the way we had come, the steamer stopping en route to pick up a night's catch of one of the salmon wheels on the river, and to deliver it at a cannery downstream.

When the proprietor of the wheel announced that his take was two thousand two hundred and thirty pounds' weight of fish, "and not a heavy catch, neither," I thought he lied. But he sent the boxes aboard, and I counted the salmon by the hundred—huge fifty-pounders, hardly dead, scores of twenty and thirty-pounders, and a host of smaller fish.

The steamer halted at a rude wooden warehouse built on piles in a lonely reach of the river, and sent in the fish. I followed them up a scale-strewn, fishy incline that led to the cannery. The crazy building was quivering with the machinery on its floors, and a glittering bank of tin-scraps twenty feet high showed where the waste was thrown after the cans had been punched. Only Chinamen were employed on the work, and they looked like blood-besmeared yellow devils, as they crossed the rifts of sun-

59

light that lay upon the floor. When our consignment arrived, the wooden boxes broke of themselves as they were dumped down under a jet of water, and the salmon burst out in a stream of quick-silver. A Chinaman jerked up a twenty-pounder, beheaded and detailed it with two swift strokes of a knife, flicked out its internal arrangements with a third, and cast it into a bloody dyed tank. The headless fish leaped from under his hands as though they were facing a rapid. Other Chinamen pulled them from the vat and thrust them under a thing like a chaffcutter, which, descending, hewed them into unseemly red gobbets fit for the can. More Chinamen with yellow, crooked fingers, jammed the stuff into the cans, which slid down some marvelous machine forthwith, soldering their own tops as they passed. Each can was hastily tested for flaws, and then sunk, with a hundred companions, into a vat of boiling water, there to be half cooked for a few minutes. The cans bulged slightly after the operation, and were therefore slidden along by the trolleyful to men with needles and soldering irons, who vented them, and soldered the aperture. Except for the label, the "finest Columbia salmon" was ready for the market. I was impressed, not so much with the speed of the manufacture, as the character of the factory. Inside, on a floor ninety by forty, the most civilized and murderous of machinery. Outside, three foot-steps, the thick-growing pines and the immense solitude of the hills. Our steamer only stayed twenty minutes at that place, but I counted two hundred and forty finished cans, made from the catch of the previous night, ere I left the slippery, blood-stained, scale-spangled, oily floors, and the offal-smeared Chinamen.

We reached Portland, California and I, crying for salmon, and the real-estate man, to whom we had been intrusted by "Portland" the insurance man, met us in the street saying that fifteen miles away, across country, we should come upon a place called Clackamas where we might perchance find what we desired. And California, his coat-tails flying in the wind, ran to a livery stable and chartered a wagon and team forthwith. I could push the wagon about with one hand, so light was its structure. The team was purely American—that is to say, almost human in its intelligence and docility. Some one said that the roads were not good on the way to Clackamas and warned us against smashing the springs. "Portland," who had watched the preparations, finally reckoned "he'd come along too," and under heavenly skies we three companions of a day set forth; California carefully lashing our rods into the carriage, and the bystanders overwhelming us with directions as to the sawmills we were to pass, the ferries we were to cross, and the sign-posts we were to seek signs from. Half a mile from this city of fifty thousand souls we struck (and this must be taken literally) a plank-road that would have been a disgrace to an Irish village.

Then six miles of macadamized road showed us that the team could move. A railway ran between us and the banks of the Willamette, and another above us through the mountains. All the land was dotted with small townships, and the roads were full of farmers in their town wagons, bunches of tow-haired, boggle-eyed urchins sitting in the hay behind. The men generally looked like loafers, but their women were all well dressed. Brown hussar-braiding on a tailor-made jacket does not, however, consort with hay-wagons. Then we struck into the woods along what California called a *"camina reale,"* — a good road, — and Portland a "fair track." It wound in and out among fire-blackened stumps, under pine trees, along the corners of log-fences, through hollows which must be hopeless marsh in the winter, and up absurd gradients. But nowhere throughout its length did I see any evidence of road-making. There was a track, — you couldn't well get off it, — and it was all you could do to stay on it. The dust lay a foot thick in the blind ruts, and under the dust we found bits of planking and bundles of brushwood that sent the wagon bounding into the air. Sometimes we crashed through bracken; anon where the blackberries grew rankest we found a lonely little cemetery, the wooden rails all awry, and the pitiful stumpy headstones nodding drunkenly at the soft green mulleins. Then with oaths and the sound of rent underwood a yoke of mighty bulls would swing down a "skid" road, hauling a forty-foot log along a rudely made slide. A valley full of wheat and cherry trees succeeded, and halting at a house we bought ten pounds weight of luscious black cherries for something less than a rupee and

61

got a drink of icy-cold water for nothing, while the untended team browsed sagaciously by the roadside. Once we found a wayside camp of horsedealers lounging by a pool, ready for a sale or a swap, and once two sun-tanned youngsters shot down a hill on Indian ponies, their full creels banging from the high-pommeled saddles. They had been fishing, and were our brethren therefore. We shouted aloud in chorus to scare a wild-cat; we squabbled over the reasons that had led a snake to cross a road; we heaved bits of bark at a venturesome chipmunk, who was really the little gray squirrel of India and had come to call on me; we lost our way and got the wagon so beautifully fixed on a steep road that we had to tie the two hind-wheels to get it down. Above all, California told tales of Nevada and Arizona, of lonely nights spent out prospecting, of the slaughter of deer and the chase of men; of woman, lovely woman, who is a firebrand in a Western city, and leads to the popping of pistols, and of the sudden changes and chances of Fortune, who delights in making the miner or the lumberman a quadruplicate millionaire, and in "busting" the railroad king. That was a day to be remembered, and it had only begun when we drew rein at a tiny farmhouse on the banks of the Clackamas and sought horse-feed and lodging ere we hastened to the river that broke over a weir not a quarter of a mile away.

Imagine a stream seventy yards broad divided by a pebbly island, running over seductive riffles, and swirling into deep, quiet pools where the good salmon goes to smoke his pipe after meals. Set such a stream amid fields of breast-high crops surrounded by hills of pine, throw in where you please quiet water, log-fenced meadows, and a hundred-foot bluff just to keep the scenery from growing too monotonous, and you will get some faint notion of the Clackamas.

Portland had no rod. He held the gaff and the whisky. California sniffed, upstream and downstream across the racing water, chose his ground, and let the gaudy spoon drop in the tail of a riffle. I was getting my rod together when I heard the joyous shriek of the reel and the yells of California, and three feet of living silver leaped into the air far across the water. The forces were engaged. The salmon tore up stream, the tense line cutting the water like a tide-rip behind him, and the light bamboo bowed to breaking. What happened after I cannot tell. California swore and prayed, and Portland shouted advice, and I did all three for what appeared to be half a day, but was in reality a little over a quarter of an hour, and sullenly our fish came home with spurts of temper, dashes head-on, and sarabands in the air; but home to the bank came he, and the remorseless reel gathered up the thread of his life inch by inch. We landed him in a little bay, and the spring-weight checked at eleven and a half pounds. Eleven and one-half pounds of fighting salmon! We danced a war-dance on the pebbles, and California caught me round the waist in a hug that went near to breaking my ribs while he shouted: "Partner! Partner! This is glory! Now you catch your fish! Twenty-four years I've waited for this!"

I went into that icy-cold river and made my cast just above a weir, and all but foul-hooked a blue and black water-snake with a coral mouth who coiled herself on a stone and hissed maledictions. The next cast—ah, the pride of it, the regal splendor of it! the thrill that ran down from finger-tip to toe! The water boiled. He broke for the fly and got it! There remained enough sense in me to give him all he wanted when he jumped not once but twenty times before the upstream flight that ran my line out to the last half-dozen turns, and I saw the nickeled reel-bar glitter under the thinning green coils. My thumb was burned deep when I strove to stopper the line, but I did not feel it till later, for my soul was out in the dancing water praying for him to turn ere he took my tackle away. The prayer was heard. As I bowed back, the butt of the rod on my left hip-bone and the top joint dipping like unto a weeping willow, he turned, and I accepted each inch of slack that I could by any means get in as a favor from on High. There be several sorts of success in this world that taste well in the moment of enjoyment, but I question whether the stealthy theft of line from an able-bodied salmon who knows exactly what you are doing and why you are doing it is not sweeter than any other victory within human scope. Like California's fish, he ran at me head-on and leaped against the line, but the Lord gave me two hundred and fifty pairs of fingers in that hour. The banks and the pine trees danced dizzily round me, but I only reeled—reeled as for life—reeled for hours, and at the end of the reeling continued to give him the butt while he sulked in a pool. California was farther up the reach, and with the corner of my eye I could see him casting with long casts and much skill. Then he struck, and my fish broke for the weir at the same instant, and down the reach we came, California and I; reel answering reel, even as the morning stars sung together.

The first wild enthusiasm of capture had died away. We were both at work now in deadly earnest to prevent the lines fouling, to stall off a downstream rush for deep water just above the weir, and at the same time to get the fish into the shallow bay downstream that gave the best practicable landing. Portland bade us both be of good heart, and volunteered to take the rod from my hands. I would rather have died among the pebbles than surrender my right to play and land my first salmon, weight unknown, on an eight-ounce rod. I heard California, at my ear it seemed, gasping: "He's a fighter from Fightersville, sure!" as his fish made a fresh break across the stream. I saw Portland fall off a log fence, break the overhanging bank, and clatter down to the pebbles, all sand and landing-net, and I dropped on a log to rest for a moment. As I drew breath the weary hands slackened their hold, and I forgot to give him the butt. A wild scutter in the water, a plunge and a break for the headwaters of the Clackamas was my reward, and the hot toil of reeling-in with one eye under the water and the other on the top joint of the rod, was renewed. Worst of all, I was blocking California's path to the little landing-bay aforesaid, and he had to halt and tire his prize where he was. "The Father of all Salmon!" he shouted. "For the love of Heaven, get your *trout* to bank, Johnny Bull." But I could no more. Even the insult failed to move me. The rest of the game was with the salmon. He suffered himself to be drawn, skipping with pretended delight at getting to the haven where I would fain have him. Yet no sooner did he feel shoal water under his ponderous belly than he backed like a torpedo-boat, and the snarl of the reel told me that my labor was in vain. A dozen times at least this happened ere the line hinted he had given up that battle and would be towed in. He was towed. The landing-net was useless for one of his size, and I would not have him gaffed. I stepped into the shallows and heaved him out with a respectful hand under the gill, for which kindness he battered me about the legs with his tail, and I felt the strength of him and was proud. California had taken my place in the shallows, his fish hard held. I was up the bank lying full length on the sweet-scented grass, and gasping in company with my first salmon caught, played and landed on an eight-ounce rod. My hands were cut and bleeding. I was dripping with sweat, spangled like harlequin with scales, wet from the waist down, nose peeled by the sun, but utterly, supremely, and consummately happy. He, the beauty, the darling, the daisy, my Salmon Bahadur, weighed twelve pounds, and I had been seven and thirty minutes bringing him to bank! He had been lightly hooked on the angle of the right jaw, and the hook had not wearied him. That hour I sat among princes and crowned heads—greater than them all. Below the bank we heard California scuffling with his salmon, and swearing Spanish oaths. Portland and I assisted at the capture, and the fish dragged the spring-balance out by the roots. It was only constructed to weigh up to fifteen pounds. We stretched the three fish on the grass,—the eleven and a half, the twelve, and fifteen pounder,—and we swore an oath that all who came after should merely be weighed and put back again.

How shall I tell the glories of that day so that you may be interested? Again and again did California and I prance down that reach to the little bay, each with a salmon in tow, and land him in the shallows. Then Portland took my rod, and caught some ten-pounders, and my spoon was carried away by an unknown leviathan. Each fish, for the merits of the three that had died so gamely, was hastily hooked on the balance and flung back, Portland recorded the weight in a pocket-book, for he was a real-estate man. Each fish fought for all he was worth, and none more savagely than the smallest—a game little six-pounder. At the end of six hours we added up the list. Total: 16 fish, aggregate weight 142 lbs. The score in detail runs something like this

—it is only interesting to those concerned: 15, 11½, 12, 10, 9¾, 8, and so forth; as I have said, nothing under six pounds, and three ten-pounders.

Very solemnly and thankfully we put up our rods—it was glory enough for all time—and returned weeping in each other's arms —weeping tears of pure joy—to that simple bare-legged family in the packing-case house by the waterside.

The old farmer recollected days and nights of fierce warfare with the Indians—"way back in the fifties," when every ripple of the Columbia River and her tributaries hid covert danger. God had dowered him with a queer crooked gift of expression, and a fierce anxiety for the welfare of his two little sons—tanned and reserved children who attended school daily, and spoke good English in a strange tongue.

His wife was an austere woman who had once been kindly and perhaps handsome.

Many years of toil had taken the elasticity out of step and voice. She looked for nothing better than everlasting work—the chafing detail of housework, and then a grave somewhere up the hill among the blackberries and the pines. But in her grim way she sympathized with her eldest daughter, a small and silent maiden of eighteen, who had thoughts very far from the meals she tended or the pans she scoured.

We stumbled into the household at a crisis; and there was a deal of downright humanity in that same. A bad, wicked dressmaker had promised the maiden a dress in time for a to-morrow's railway journey, and, though the barefooted Georgie, who stood in very wholesome awe of his sister, had scoured the woods on a pony in search, that dress never arrived. So with sorrow in her heart, and a hundred Sister Anne glances up the road, she waited upon the strangers, and I doubt not, cursed them for the wants that stood between her and her need for tears. It was a genuine little tragedy. The mother in a heavy, passionless voice rebuked her impatience, yet sat bowed over a heap of sewing for the daughter's benefit.

These things I beheld in the long marigold-scented twilight and whispering night, loafing round the little house with California, who unfolded himself like a lotus to the moon; or in the little boarded bunk that was our bedroom, swapping tales with Portland and the old man. Most of the yarns began in this way:

"Red Larry was a bull-puncher back of Lone County, Montana," or "There was a man riding the trail met a jack-rabbit sitting in a cactus," or "'Bout the time of the San Diego land boom, a woman from Monterey." etc.

You can try to piece out for yourselves what sort of stories they were.

And next day California took me under his wing and told me we were going to see a city smitten by a boom, and catch trout. So we took a train and killed a cow—she wouldn't get out of the way, and the locomotive "chanced" her and slew—and crossing into Washington Territory won the town of Tacoma, which stands at the head of Puget Sound upon the road to Alaska and Vancouver.

California was right. Tacoma was literally staggering under a boom of the boomiest. I do not quite remember what her natural resources were supposed to be, though every second man shrieked a selection in my ear. They included coal and iron, carrots, potatoes, lumber, shipping, and a crop of thin newspapers all telling Portland that her days were numbered. California and I struck the place at twilight. The rude boarded pavements of the main streets rumbled under the heels of hundreds of furious men all actively engaged in hunting drinks and eligible corner-lots. They sought the drinks first. The street itself alternated five-story business blocks of the later and more abominable forms of architecture with board shanties. Overhead the drunken telegraph, telephone, electric light wires tangled on the tottering posts whose butts were half-whittled through by the knife of the loafer. Down the muddy, grimy, unmetaled thoroughfare ran a horse-car line— the metals three inches above road level. Beyond this street rose many hills, and the town was thrown like a broken set of dominoes over all. A steam tramway—it left the track the only time I used it—was nosing about the hills, but the most prominent features of the landscape were the foundations in brick and stone of a gigantic opera house and the blackened stumps of the pines. California sized up the town with one comprehensive glance. "Big boom," said he; and a few instants later: "About time to step off, I think," meaning thereby that the boom had risen to its limit, and it would be expedient not to meddle with it. We passed down ungraded streets that ended abruptly in a fifteen-foot drop and a nest of brambles; along pavements that beginning in pine-plank ended in the living tree; by hotels with Turkish mosque trinketry on their shameless tops, and the pine stumps at their very doors; by a female seminary, tall, gaunt and red, which a native of the town bade us marvel at, and we marveled; by houses built in imitation of the ones on Nob Hill, San Francisco,—after the Dutch fashion; by other houses, plenteously befouled with jig-saw work, and others flaring with the castlemented, battlemented bosh of the wooden Gothic school.

"You can tell just about when those fellers had their houses built," quoth California. "That one yonder wanted to be *I*talian, and his architect built him what he wanted. The new houses with the low straddle roofs and windows pitched in sideways and red brick walls are Dutch. That's the latest idea. I can read the history of the town." I had no occasion so to read. The natives were only too glad and too proud to tell me. The hotel walls bore a flaming panorama of Tacoma in which by the eye of faith I saw a faint resemblance to the real town. The hotel stationery advertised that Tacoma bore on its face all the advantages of the highest civilization, and the newspapers sang the same tune in a louder key. The real-estate agents were selling house-lots on unmade streets miles away for thousands of dollars. On the streets —the rude, crude streets, where the unshaded electric light was fighting with the gentle northern twilight—men were babbling of money, town lots, and again money—how Alf or Ed had done such and such a thing that had brought him so much money; and round the corner in a creaking boarded hall the red-jerseyed Salvationists were calling upon mankind to renounce all and follow their noisy God. The men dropped in by twos and threes, listened silently for a while, and as silently went their way, the cymbals clashing after them in vain. I think it was the raw, new smell of fresh saw-dust everywhere pervading the air that threw upon me a desolating homesickness. It brought back in a moment all remembrances of that terrible first night at school when the establishment has been newly whitewashed, and a soft smell of escaping gas mingles with the odor of trunks and wet overcoats. I was a little boy, and the school was very new. A vagabond among collarless vagabonds, I loafed up the street, looking into the fronts of little shops where they sold slop shirts at fancy prices, which shops I saw later described in the papers as "great." California had gone off to investigate on his own account, and presently returned, laughing noiselessly. "They are all mad here," he said, "all mad. A man nearly pulled a gun on me because I didn't agree with him that Tacoma was going to whip San Francisco on the strength of carrots and potatoes. I asked him to tell me what the town produced, and I couldn't get anything out of him except those two darned vegetables. Say, what do you think?"

I responded firmly, "I'm going into British territory a little while—to draw breath."

"I'm going up the Sound, too, for a while," said he, "but I'm coming back—coming back to our salmon on the Clackamas. A man has been pressing me to buy real estate here. Young feller, don't you buy real estate here."

California disappeared with a kindly wave of his overcoat into worlds other than mine,—good luck go with him, for he was a true sportsman!—and I took a steamer up Puget Sound for Vancouver, which is the terminus of the Canadian Pacific Railway. That was a queer voyage. The water, landlocked among a thousand islands, lay still as oil under our bows, and the wake of the screw broke up the unquivering reflections of pines and cliffs a mile away. 'Twas as though we were trampling on glass. No one, not even the Government, knows the number of islands in the Sound. Even now you can get one almost for the asking; can build a house, raise sheep, catch Salmon, and become a king on a small scale—your subjects the Indians of the reservation, who glide among the islets in their canoes and scratch their hides monkey-wise by the beach. A Sound Indian is unlovely, and only by accident picturesque. His wife drives the canoe, but he himself is so thorough a mariner that he can spring up in his cockle-craft and whack his wife over the head with a paddle without tipping the whole affair into the water. This I have seen him do unprovoked. I fancy it must have been to show off before the whites.

Have I told you anything about Seattle—the town that was burned out a few weeks ago when the insurance men at San Francisco took their losses with a grin? In the ghostly twilight, just as the forest fires were beginning to glare from the unthrifty islands, we struck it—struck it heavily, for the wharves had all been burned down, and we tied up where we could, crashing into the rotten foundations of a boat house as a pig roots in high grass. The town, like Tacoma, was built upon a hill. In the heart of the business quarters there was a horrible black smudge, as though a Hand had come down and rubbed the place smooth. I know now what being wiped out means. The smudge seemed to be about a mile long, and its blackness was relieved by tents in which men were doing business with the wreck of the stock they had saved. There were shouts and counter-shouts from the steamer to the temporary wharf, which was laden with shingles for roofing, chairs, trunks, provision-boxes, and all the lath and string arrangements out of which a western town is made. This is the way the shouts ran:—

"Oh, George! What's the best with you?"

"Nawthin'. Got the old safe out. She's burned to a crisp. Books all gone."

"Save anythin'?"

"Bar'l o' crackers and my wife's bonnet. Goin' to start store on them though."

"Bully for you. Where's that Emporium? I'll drop in."

"Corner what used to be Fourth and Main—little brown tent close to militia picket. Sa-ay! We're under martial law, an' all the saloons are shut down."

"Best for you, George. Some men gets crazy with a fire, an' liquor makes 'em crazier."

"'Spect any creator-condemned son of a female dog who has

lost all his fixin's in a conflagration is going to put ice on his head an' run for Congress, do you? How'd you like us act?"

The Job's comforter on the steamer retired into himself.

"Oh, George" dived into the bar for a drink.

P.S. — Among many curiosities I have unearthed one. It was a Face on a steamer — a face above a pointed straw-colored beard, a face with thin lips and eloquent eyes. We conversed, and presently I got at the ideas of the Face. It was, though it lived for nine months of the year in the wilds of Alaska and British Columbia, an authority on the canon law of the Church of England — a zealous and bitter upholder of the supremacy of the aforesaid Church. Into my amazed ears, as the steamer plodded through the reflections of the stars, it poured the battle-cry of the Church Militant here on earth, and put forward as a foul injustice that in the prisons of British Columbia the Protestant chaplain did not always belong to the Church. The Face had no official connection with the august body, and by force of his life very seldom attended service.

"But," said he, proudly, "I should think it direct disobedience to the orders of my Church if I attended any other places of worship than those prescribed. I was once for three months in a place where there was only a Wesleyan Methodist chapel, and I never set foot in it once, Sir. Never once. 'Twould have been heresy. Rank heresy."

And as I leaned over the rail methought that all the little stars in the water were shaking with austere merriment! But it may have been only the ripple of the steamer, after all.

VII

"But who shall chronicle the ways
Of common folk, the nights and days
Spent with rough goatherds on the snows,
And travelers come whence no man knows?"

This day I know how a deserter feels. Here in Victoria, a hundred
and forty miles out of America, the mail brings me news from our
Home—the land of regrets. I was enjoying myself by the side of a
trout-stream, and I feel inclined to apologize for every rejoicing
breath I drew in the diamond clear air. The sickness, they said,
is heavy with you; from Rewari to the south good men are dying.
Two names come in by the mail of two strong men dead—men
that I dined and jested with only a little time ago, and it seems
unfair that I should be here, cut off from the chain-gang and the
shot-drill of our weary life. After all, there is no life like it that
we lead over yonder. Americans are Americans, and there are
millions of them; English are English; but we of India are Us all
the world over, knowing the mysteries of each other's lives and
sorrowing for the death of a brother. How can I sit down and
write to you of the mere joy of being alive? The news has killed
the pleasure of the day for me, and I am ashamed of myself. There
are seventy brook trout lying in a creel, fresh drawn from Harrison
Hot Springs, and they do not console me. They are like the stolen
apples that clinch the fact of a bad boy's playing truant. I would
sell them all, with my heritage in the woods and air and the delight
of meeting new and strange people, just to be back again in the
old galling harness, the heat and the dust, the gatherings in the
evenings by the flooded tennis-courts, the ghastly dull dinners at
the Club when the very last woman has been packed off to the
hills and the four or five surviving men ask the doctor the symp-

toms of incubating smallpox. I should be troubled in body, but at peace in the soul. O excellent and toil-worn public of mine—men of the brotherhood, griffins new joined from the February troopers, and gentlemen waiting for your off reckonings—take care of yourselves and keep well! It hurts so when any die. There are so few of Us, and we know one another too intimately.

*

Vancouver three years ago was swept off by fire in sixteen minutes, and only one house was left standing. To-day it has a population of fourteen thousand people, and builds it houses out of brick with dressed granite fronts. But a great sleepiness lies on Vancouver as compared with an American town; men don't fly up and down the streets telling lies, and the spittoons in the delightfully comfortable hotel are unused; the baths are free and their doors are unlocked. You do not have to dig up the hotel clerk when you want to bathe, which shows the inferiority of Vancouver. An American bade me notice the absence of bustle, and was alarmed when in a loud and audible voice I thanked God for it. "Give me granite—hewn granite and peace," quoth I, "and keep your deal boards and bustle for yourselves."

The Canadian Pacific terminus is not a very gorgeous place as yet, but you can be shot directly from the window of the train into the liner that will take you in fourteen days from Vancouver to Yokohama. The *Parthia,* of some five thousand tons, was at her berth when I came, and the sight of the ex-Cunard on what seemed to be a little lake was curious. Except for certain currents which are not much mentioned, but which make the entrance rather unpleasant for sailing-boats, Vancouver possesses an almost perfect harbor. The town is built all round and about the harbor, and young as it is, its streets are better than those of western America. Moreover, the old flag waves over some of the buildings, and this is cheering to the soul. The place is full of Englishmen who speak the English tongue correctly and with clearness, avoiding more blasphemy than is necessary, and taking a respectable length of time to getting outside their drinks. These advantages and others that I have heard about, such as the construction of elaborate workshops and the like by the Canadian Pacific in the near future, moved me to invest in real estate. He that sold it me was a delightful English Boy who, having tried for the Army and failed, had somehow meandered into a real-estate office, where he was doing well. I couldn't have bought it from an American. He would have overstated the case and proved me the possessor of the original Eden. All the Boy said was: "I give you my word it isn't on a cliff or under water, and before long the town ought to move out that way. I'd advise you to take it." And I took it as easily as a man buys a piece of tobacco. *Me voici,* owner of some four hundred well developed pines, a few thousand tons of granite scattered in blocks at the roots of the pines, and a sprinkling of earth. That's a town-lot in Vancouver. You or your agent hold to it till property rises, then sell out and buy more land further out of town and repeat the process. I do not quite see how this sort of thing helps the growth of a town, but the English Boy says that it is the "essence of speculation," so it must be all right. But I wish there were fewer pines and rather less granite on my ground. Moved by curiosity and the lust of trout, I went seventy miles up the Canadian Pacific in one of the cross-Continent cars, which are cleaner and less stuffy than the Pullman. A man who goes all the way across Canada is liable to be disappointed—not in the scenery, but in the progress of the country. So a batch of wandering politicians from England told me. They even went so far as to say that Eastern Canada was a failure and unprofitable. The place didn't move, they complained, and whole counties—they said provinces—lay under the rule of the Roman Catholic priests, who took care that the people should not be over-cumbered with the good things of this world to the detriment of their souls. My interest was in the line—the real and accomplished railway which is to throw actual fighting troops into the East some day when our hold of the Suez Canal is temporarily loosened.

All that Vancouver wants is a fat earthwork fort upon a hill,— there are plenty of hills to choose from,—a selection of big guns, a couple of regiments of infantry, and later on a big arsenal. The raw self-consciousness of America would be sure to make her think these arrangements intended for her benefit, but she could be enlightened. It is not seemly to leave unprotected the head-end of a big railway; for though Victoria and Esquimalt, our naval stations on Vancouver Island, are very near, so also is a place called Vladivostok, and though Vancouver Narrows are strait, they allow room enough for a man-of-war. The people—I did not speak to more than two hundred of them—do not know about Russia or military arrangements. They are trying to open trade with Japan in lumber, and are raising fruit, wheat, and sometimes minerals. All of them agree that we do not yet know the resources of British Columbia, and all joyfully bade me note the climate, which was distinctly warm. "We never have killing cold here. It's the most perfect climate in the world." Then there are three perfect climates, for I have tasted 'em—California, Washington Territory, and British Columbia. I cannot say which is the loveliest.

When I left by steamer and struck across the Sound to our naval station at Victoria, Vancouver Island, I found in that quite English town of beautiful streets quite a colony of old men doing nothing but talking, fishing, and loafing at the Club. That means that the retired go to Victoria. On a thousand a year pension a man would be a millionaire in these parts, and for four hundred he could live well. It was at Victoria they told me the tale of the fire in Vancouver. How the inhabitants of New Westminster, twelve miles from Vancouver, saw a glare in the sky at six in the evening, but thought it was a forest fire; how later bits of burnt paper flew about their streets, and they guessed that evil had happened; how an hour later a man rode into the city crying that there was no Vancouver left. All had been wiped out by the flames in sixteen minutes. How, two hours later, the Mayor of New Westminster having voted nine thousand dollars from the Municipal funds, relief-wagons with food and blankets were pouring into where Vancouver stood. How fourteen people were supposed to have died in the fire, but how even now when they laid new foundations the workmen unearthed charred skeletons, many more than fourteen. "That night," said the teller, "all Vancouver was houseless. The wooden town had gone in a breath. Next day they began to build in brick, and you have seen what they have achieved."

The sight afar off of three British men-of-war and a torpedo-boat consoled me as I returned from Victoria to Tacoma and discovered *en route* that I was surfeited with scenery. There is a great deal in the remark of a discontented traveler: "When you have seen a fine forest, a bluff, a river, and a lake you have seen all the scenery of western America. Sometimes the pine is three hundred feet high, and sometimes the rock is, and sometimes the lake is a hundred miles long. But it's all the same, don't you know. I'm getting sick of it." I dare not say getting sick. I'm only tired. If Providence could distribute all this beauty in little bits where people most wanted it—among you in India,—it would be well. But it is en masse, overwhelming, with nobody but the tobacco-chewing captain of a river steamboat to look at it. Men said if I went to Alaska I should see islands even more wooded, snow-peaks loftier, and rivers more lovely than those around me. That decided me not to go to Alaska. I went east—east to Montana, after another horrible night in Tacoma among the men who spat. Why does the Westerner spit? It can't amuse him, and it doesn't interest his neighbor.

But I am beginning to mistrust. Everything good as well as everything bad is supposed to come from the East. Is there a shooting-scrape between prominent citizens? Oh, you'll find nothing of that kind in the East. Is there a more than usually revolting lynching? They don't do that in the East. I shall find out when I get there whether this unnatural perfection be real.

Eastward then to Montana I took my way for the Yellowstone National Park, called in the guide-books "Wonderland." But the real Wonderland began in the train. We were a merry crew. One gentleman announced his intention of paying no fare and grappled the conductor, who neatly cross-buttocked him through a double plate-glass window. His head was cut open in four or five places. A doctor on the train hastily stitched up the biggest gash, and he was dropped at a wayside station, spurting blood at every hair—a scarlet-headed and ghastly sight. The conductor guessed that he would die, and volunteered the information that there was no profit in monkeying with the North Pacific Railway.

Night was falling when we cleared the forests and sailed out upon a wilderness of sage brush. The desolation of Montgomery, the wilderness of Sind, the hummock-studded desert of Bikaneer, are joyous and homelike compared to the impoverished misery of the sage. It is blue, it is stunted, it is dusty. It wraps the rolling hills as a mildewed shroud wraps the body of a long-dead man. It makes you weep for sheer loneliness, and there is no getting away from it. When Childe Roland came to the dark Tower he traversed the sage brush.

Yet there is one thing worse than sage unadulterated and that is a prairie city. We stopped at Pasco Junction, and a man told me that it was the Queen City of the Prairie. I wish Americans didn't tell such useless lies. I counted fourteen or fifteen frame-houses, and a portion of a road that showed like a bruise on the untouched surface of the blue sage, running away and away up to the setting sun. The sailor sleeps with a half-inch plank between himself and death. He is at home beside the handful of people who curl themselves up o'nights with nothing but a frail scantling, almost as thin as a blanket, to shut out the unmeasurable loneliness of the sage.

When the train stopped on the road, as it did once or twice, the solid silence of the sage got up and shouted at us. It was like a nightmare, and one not in the least improved by having to sleep in an emigrant-car; the regularly ordained sleepers being full. There was a row in our car toward morning, a man having managed to get querulously drunk in the night. Up rose a Cornishman with a red head full of strategy, and strapped the obstreperous one, smiling largely as he did so, and a delicate little woman in a far bunk watched the fray and called the drunken man a "damned hog," which he certainly was, though she needn't have put it quite so coarsely. Emigrant cars are clean, but the accommodation is as hard as a plank bed.

Later we laid our bones down to crossing the Rockies. An American train can climb up the side of a house if need be, but it is not pleasant to sit in it. We clomb till we struck violent cold and an Indian Reservation, and the noble savage came to look at us. He was a Flathead and unlovely. Most Americans are charmingly frank about the Indian. "Let us get rid of him as soon as possible," they say. "We have no use for him." Some of the men I meet have a notion that we in India are exterminating the native in the same fashion, and I have been asked to fix a date for the final extinguishment of the Aryan. I answer that it will be a long business. Very many Americans have an offensive habit of referring to natives as "heathen." Mahometans and Hindus are heathen alike in their eyes, and they vary the epithet with "pagan" and "idolater." But this is beside the matter, which is the Stampede Tunnel—our actual point of crossing the Rockies. Thank Heaven, I need never take that tunnel again! It is about two miles long, and in effect is nothing more than the gallery of a mine shored with timber and lighted with electric lamps. Black darkness would be preferable, for the lamps just reveal the rough cutting of the rocks, and that is very rough indeed. The train crawls through, brakes down, and you can hear the water and little bits of stone falling on the roof of the car. Then you pray, pray fervently, and the air gets stiller and stiller, and you dare not take your unwilling eyes off the timber shoring, lest a prop should fall for lack of your moral support. Before the tunnel was built you crossed in the open air by a switch-back line. A watchman goes through the tunnel, after each train, but that is no protection. He just guesses that another train will pull through, and the engine-driver guesses the same thing. Some day between the two of them there will be a cave-in in the tunnel. Then the enterprising reporter will talk about the shrieks and groans of the buried and the heroic efforts of the Press in securing first information, and—that will be all. Human life is of small account out here.

I was listening to yarns in the smoking-compartment of the Pullman, all the way to Helena, and with very few exceptions, each had for its point, violent, brutal, and ruffianly murder— murder by fraud and the craft of the savage—murder unavenged by the law, or at the most by an outbreak of fresh lawlessness. At the end of each tale I was assured that the old days had passed away, and that these were anecdotes of five years' standing. One man in particular distinguished himself by holding up to admiration the exploits of some cowboys of his acquaintance, and their skill in the use of the revolver. Each tale of horror wound up with "and that's the sort of man he was," as who should say: "Go and do likewise." Remember that the shootings, the cuttings, and the stabbings were not the outcome of any species of legitimate warfare; the heroes were not forced to fight for their lives. Far from it. The brawls were bred by liquor in which they assisted— in saloons and gambling-hells they were wont to "pull their guns" on a man, and in the vast majority of cases without provocation. The tales sickened me, but taught one thing. A man who carries a pistol may be put down as a coward—a person to be shut out from every decent mess and club, and gathering of civilized folk. There is neither chivalry nor romance in the weapon, for all that American authors have seen fit to write. I would I could make you understand the full measure of contempt which certain aspects of Western life have inspired me. Let us try a comparison. Sometimes it happens that a young, a very young, man, whose first dress-coat is yet glossy, gets slightly flushed at a dinner-party among his seniors. After the ladies are gone, he begins to talk. He talks, you will remember, as a "man of the world" and a person of varied experiences, an authority on all things human and divine. The gray heads of the elders bow assentingly to his wildest statement; some one tries to turn the conversation when what the youngster conceives to be wit has offended a sensibility; and another deftly slides the decanters beyond him as they circle round the table. You know the feeling of discomfort—pity mingled with aversion—over the boy who is making an exhibition of himself. The same emotion came back to me, when an old man who ought to have known better appealed from time to time for admiration of his pitiful sentiments. It was right in his mind to insult, to maim, and to kill; right to evade the law where it was strong and to trample over it where it was weak; right to swindle in politics, to lie in affairs of State, and commit perjury in matters of municipal administration. The car was full of little children, utterly regardless of their parents, fretful, peevish, spoilt beyond anything I have ever seen in Anglo-India. They in time would grow up into men such as sat in the smoker, and had no regard for the law, men who would conduct papers siding "with defiance of any and every law." But it's of no consequence, as Mr. Toots says.

During the descent of the Rockies we journeyed for a season on a trestle only two hundred and eighty-six feet high. It was made of iron, but up till two years ago a wooden structure bore up the train, and was used long after it had been condemned by the civil engineers. Some day the iron one will come down, just as Stampede Tunnel will, and the results will be even more startling.

Late in the night we ran over a skunk—ran over it in the dark. Everything that has been said about the skunk is true. It is an Awesome Stink.

VIII

Livingston is a town of two thousand people, and the junction for the little side-line that takes you to the Yellowstone National Park. It lies in a fold of the prairie, and behind it is the Yellowstone River and the gate of the mountains through which the river flows. There is one street in the town, where the cowboy's pony and the little foal of the brood-mare in the buggy rest contentedly in the blinding sunshine while the cowboy gets himself shaved at the only other barber's shop, and swaps lies at the bar. I exhausted the town, including the saloons, in ten minutes, and got away on the rolling grass downs where I threw myself to rest. Directly under the hill I was on, swept a drove of horses in charge of two mounted men. That was a picture I shall not soon forget. A light haze of dust went up from the hoof-trodden green, scarcely veiling the unfettered deviltries of three hundred horses who very much wanted to stop and graze. "Yow! Yow! Yow!" yapped the mounted men in chorus like coyotes. The column moved forward at a trot, divided as it met a hillock and scattered into fan shape all among the suburbs of Livingston. I heard the "snick" of a stock whip, half a dozen "Yow, yows," and the mob had come together again, and, with neighing and wickering and squealing and a great deal of kicking on the part of the youngsters, rolled like a wave of brown water toward the uplands.

I was within twenty feet of the leader, a gray stallion—lord of many brood-mares all deeply concerned for the welfare of their fuzzy foals. A cream-colored beast—I knew him at once for the bad character of the troop—broke back, taking with him some frivolous fillies. I heard the snick of the whips somewhere in the dust, and the fillies came back at a canter, very shocked and indignant. On the heels of the last rode both the stockmen— picturesque ruffians who wanted to know "what in hell" I was doing there, waved their hats, and swept down the slope after their charges. When the noise of the troop had died there came a wonderful silence on all the prairie—that silence, they say, which enters into the heart of the old-time hunter and trapper and marks him off from the rest of his race. The town disappeared in the darkness, and a very young moon showed herself over a bald-headed, snow-flecked peak. Then the Yellowstone, hidden by the water-willows, lifted up its voice and sang a little song to the mountains, and an old horse that had crept up in the dusk breathed inquiringly on the back of my neck. When I reached the hotel I found all manner of preparation under way for the 4th of July, and a drunken man with a Winchester rifle over his shoulder patrolling the sidewalk. I do not think he wanted any one. He carried the gun as other folk carry walking-sticks. None the less I avoided the direct line of fire and listened to the blasphemies of miners and stockmen till far into the night. In every bar-room lay a copy of the local paper, and every copy impressed it upon the inhabitants of Livingston that they were the best, finest, bravest, richest, and most progressive town of the most progressive nation under Heaven; even as Tacoma and Portland papers had belauded their readers. And yet, all my purblind eyes could see was a grubby little hamlet full of men without clean collars and perfectly unable to get through one sentence unadorned by three oaths. They raise horses and minerals round and about Livingston, but they behave as though they raised cherubims with diamonds in their wings.

From Livingston the National Park train follows the Yellowstone River through the gate of the mountains and over arid volcanic country. A stranger in the cars saw me look at the ideal trout-stream below the windows and murmured softly: "Lie off at Yankee Jim's if you want good fishing." They halted the train at the head of a narrow valley, and I leaped literally into the arms of Yankee Jim, sole owner of a log hut and an indefinite amount of hay-ground, and constructor of twenty-seven miles of wagon-road over which he held toll right. There was the hut—the river fifty yards away, and the polished line of metals that disappeared round a bluff. That was all. The railway added the finishing touch to the already complete loneliness of the place. Yankee Jim was a picturesque old man with a talent for yarns that Annanias might have envied. It seemed to me, presumptuous in my ignorance, that I might hold my own with the old-timer if I judiciously painted up a few lies gathered in the course of my wanderings. Yankee Jim saw every one of my tales and went fifty better on the spot. He dealt in bears and Indians—never less than twenty of each; had known the Yellowstone country for years; and bore upon his body marks of Indian arrows; and his eyes had seen a squaw of the Crow Indians burned alive at the stake. He said she screamed considerably. In one point did he speak the truth—as regarded the merits of that particular reach of the Yellowstone. He said it was alive with trout. It was. I fished it from noon till twilight, and the fish bit at the brown hook as though never a fat trout-fly had fallen on the water. From pebbly reaches, quivering in the heat-haze where the foot caught on stumps cut four-square by the chisel-tooth of the beaver; past the fringe of the water-willow crowded with the breeding trout-fly and alive with toads and water-snakes; over the drifted timber to the grateful shadow of the big trees that darkened the holes where the fattest fish lay, I worked for seven hours. The mountain flanks on either side of the valley gave back the heat as the desert gives it, and the dry sand by the railway track, where I found a rattlesnake, was hot-iron to the touch. But the trout did not care for the heat. They breasted the boiling river for my fly and they got it. I simply dare not give my bag. At the fortieth trout I gave up counting, and I had reached the fortieth in less than two hours. They were small fish,—not one over two pounds,—but they fought like small tigers, and I lost three flies before I could understand their methods of escape. Ye gods! That was fishing though it peeled the skin from my nose in strips.

At twilight Yankee Jim bore me off, protesting, to supper in the hut. The fish had prepared me for any surprise, wherefore when Yankee Jim introduced me to a young woman of five-and-twenty, with eyes like the deep-fringed eyes of the gazelle, and "on the neck the small head buoyant, like a bell-flower in its bed," I said nothing. It was all in the day's events. She was California-raised, the wife of a man who owned a stock-farm "up the river a little

ways," and, with her husband, tenant of Yankee Jim's shanty. I
know she wore list slippers, and did not wear stays; but I know
also that she was beautiful by any standard of beauty, and that
the trout she cooked were fit for a king's supper. And after supper
strange men loafed up in the dim delicious twilight, with the little
news of the day—how a heifer had "gone strayed" from Nichol-
son's; how the widow at Grant's Fork wouldn't part with a little
hayland nohow, though "she an' her big brothers can't manage
more than ha-af of the land now. She's so darned proud." Diana
of the Crossways entertained them in queenly wise, and her husband and Yankee Jim bade them sit right down and make themselves at home. Then did Yankee Jim uncurl his choicest lies on
Indian warfare aforetime; then did the whisky-flask circle round
the little crowd; then did Diana's husband 'low that he was quite
handy with the lariat, but had seen men rope a steer by any foot
or horn indicated: then did Diana unburden herself about her
neighbors. The nearest house was three miles away, "but the
women aren't nice, neighborly folk. They talk so. They haven't
got anything else to do, seemingly. If a woman goes to a dance
and has a good time, they talk, and if she wears a silk dress,
they want to know how just ranchin' folks—folks on a ranch—
come by such things; and they make mischief down all the lands
here from Gardiner City way back up to Livingston. They're
mostly Montana raised, and they haven't been nowheres. Ah,
how they talk!" "Were things like this," demanded Diana, "in the
big world outside, whence I had come?" "Yes," I said, "things
were very much the same all over the world," and I thought of
a far-away station in India, where new dresses and the having of
good times at dances raised cackle more grammatical perhaps,
but no less venomous than the gossip of the "Montana-raised"
folk on the ranches of the Yellowstone.

Next morn I fished again and listened to Diana telling the story
of her life. I forget what she told me, but I am distinctly aware
that she had royal eyes and a mouth that the daughter of a hundred earls might have envied—so small and so delicately cut it
was. "An' you come back an' see us again," said the simple-minded

folk. "Come back an' we'll show you how to catch six-pound trout at the head of the cañon."

To-day I am in the Yellowstone Park, and I wish I were dead. The train halted at Cinnabar station, and we were decanted, a howling crowd of us, into stages, variously horsed, for the eight-mile drive to the first spectacle of the Park—a place called the Mammoth Hot Springs. "What means this eager, anxious throng?" I asked the driver. "You've struck one of Rayment's excursion parties—that's all—a crowd of creator-condemned fools mostly. Aren't you one of 'em?" "No," I said. "May I sit up here with you, great chief and man with a golden tongue? I do not know Mister Rayment. I belong to T. Cook and Son." The other person, from the quality of the material he handles, must be the son of a sea-cook. He collects masses of Down-Easters from the New England States and elsewhere and hurls them across the Continent and into Yellowstone Park on tour. A brake-load of Cook's Continental tourists trapezing through Paris (I've seen 'em) are angels of light compared to the Rayment trippers. It is not the ghastly vulgarity, the oozing, rampant Bessemer steel self-sufficiency and ignorance of the men that revolts me, so much as the display of these same qualities in the womenfolk. I saw a new type in the coach, and all my dreams of a better and more perfect East died away. "Are these—um—persons here any sort of persons in their own places?" I asked a shepherd who appeared to be herding them.

"Why, certainly. They include very many prominent and representative citizens from seven States of the Union, and most of them are wealthy. Yes, *sir*. Representative and prominent."

We ran across the bare hills on an unmetaled road under a burning sun in front of a volley of playful repartee from the prominent citizens inside. It was the 4th of July. The horses had American flags in their headstalls, some of the women wore flags and colored handkerchiefs in their belts, and a young German on the box-seat with me was bewailing the loss of a box of crackers. He said he had been sent to the Continent to get his schooling and so had lost his American accent; but no Continental schooling writes German Jew all over a man's face and nose. He was a rabid American citizen—one of a very difficult class to deal with. As a general rule, praise unsparingly, and without discrimination. That keeps most men quiet; but some, if you fail to keep up a continuous stream of praise, proceed to revile the Old Country— Germans and Irish who are more Americans than the Americans are the chief offenders. This young American began to attack the English army. He had seen some of it on parade and he pitied the men in bearskins as "slaves." The citizen, by the way, has a contempt for his own army which exceeds anything you meet among the most illiberal classes in England. I admitted that our army was very poor, had done nothing, and had been nowhere. This exasperated him, for he expected an argument, and he trampled on the British Lion generally. Failing to move me, he vowed that I had no patriotism like his own. I said I had not, and further ventured that very few Englishmen had; which, when you come to think of it, is quite true. By the time he had proved conclusively that before the Prince of Wales came to the throne we should be a blethering republic, we struck a road that overhung a river, and my interest in "politics" was lost in admiration of the driver's skill as he sent his four big horses along the winding road. There was no room for any sort of accident—a shy or a swerve would have dropped us sixty feet into the roaring Gardiner River. Some of the persons in the coach remarked that the scenery was "elegant." Wherefore, even at the risk of my own life, I did urgently desire an accident and the massacre of some of the more prominent citizens. What "elegance" lies in a thousand-foot pile of honey-colored rock, riven into peak and battlement, the highest peak defiantly crowned by an eagle's nest, the eaglet peering into the gulf and screaming for his food, I could not for the life of me understand. But they speak a strange tongue.

En route we passed other carriages full of trippers, who had done their appointed five days in the Park, and yelped at us fraternally as they disappeared in clouds of red dust. When we struck the Mammoth Hot Spring Hotel—a huge yellow barn—a signboard informed us that the altitude was six thousand two hundred feet. The Park is just a howling wilderness of three thousand square miles, full of all imaginable freaks of a fiery nature. A hotel company, assisted by the Secretary of State for the Interior, appears to control it; there are hotels at all the points of interest, guide-books, stalls for the sale of minerals, and so forth, after the model of Swiss summer places.

The tourists—may their master die an evil death at the hand of a mad locomotive!—poured into that place with a joyful whoop, and, scarce washing the dust from themselves, began to celebrate the 4th of July. They called it "patriotic exercises;" elected a clergyman of their own faith as president, and, sitting on the landing of the first floor, began to make speeches and read the Declaration of Independence. The clergyman rose up and told them they were the greatest, freest, sublimest, most chivalrous, and richest people on the face of the earth, and they all said Amen. Another clergyman asserted in the words of the Declaration that all men were created equal, and equally entitled to Life, Liberty, and the pursuit of Happiness. I should like to know whether the wild and woolly West recognizes this first right as freely as the grantors intended. The clergyman then bade the world note that the tourists included representatives of seven of the New England States; whereat I felt deeply sorry for the New England States in their latter days. He opined that this running to and fro upon the earth, under the auspices of the excellent Rayment, would draw America more closely together, especially when the Westerners remembered the perils that they of the East had surmounted by rail and river. At duly appointed intervals the congregation sang "My country, 'tis of thee" to the tune of "God save the Queen" (here they did not stand up), and the "Star-Spangled Banner" (here they did), winding up the exercise with some doggerel of their own composition to the tune of "John Brown's body," movingly setting forth the perils before alluded to. They then adjourned to the verandas and watched fire-crackers of the feeblest, exploding one by one, for several hours.

What amazed me was the calm with which these folks gathered together and commenced to belaud their noble selves, their country, and their "institootions" and everything else that was theirs.

The language was, to these bewildered ears, wild advertisement, gas, bunkum, blow, anything you please beyond the bounds of common sense. An archangel, selling town-lots on the Glassy Sea, would have blushed to the tips of his wings to describe his property in similar terms. Then they gathered round the pastor and told him his little sermon was "perfectly glorious," really grand, sublime, and so forth, and he bridled ecclesiastically. At the end a perfectly unknown man attacked me and asked me what I thought of American Patriotism. I said there was nothing like it in the Old Country. By the way, always tell an American this. It soothes him.

Then said he: "Are you going to get out your letters—your letters of naturalization?"

"Why?" I asked.

"I presoom you do business in this country, and make money out of it,—and it seems to me that it would be your dooty."

"Sir," said I, sweetly, "there is a forgotten little isle across the seas called England. It is not much bigger than the Yellowstone Park. In that island a man of your country could work, marry, make his fortune or twenty fortunes, and die. Throughout his career not one soul would ask him whether he were a British subject or a child of the Devil. Do you understand?"

I think he did, because he said something about "Britishers" which wasn't complimentary.

IX

"That desolate land and lone
Where the Big Horn and Yellowstone
Roar down their mountain path."

Twice have I written this letter from end to end. Twice have I torn it up, fearing lest those across the water should say that I had gone mad on a sudden. Now we will begin for the third time quite solemnly and soberly. I have been through the Yellowstone National Park in a buggy, in the company of an adventurous old lady from Chicago and her husband, who disapproved of scenery as being "ongodly." I fancy it scared them.

We began, as you know, with the Mammoth Hot Springs. They are only a gigantic edition of those pink and white terraces not long ago destroyed by earthquake in New Zealand. At one end of the little valley in which the hotel stands the lime-laden springs that break from the pine-covered hillsides have formed a frozen cataract of white, lemon, and palest pink formation, through and over and in which water of the warmest bubbles and drips and trickles from pale-green lagoon to exquisitely fretted basin. The ground rings hollow as a kerosene-tin, and some day the Mammoth Hotel, guests and all, will sink into the caverns below and be turned into a stalactite. When I set foot on the first of the terraces, a tourist-trampled ramp of scabby gray stuff, I met a stream of iron-red hot water which ducked into a hole like a rabbit. Followed a gentle chuckle of laughter, and then a deep, exhausted sigh from nowhere in particular. Fifty feet above my head a jet of steam rose up and died out in the blue. It was worse than the boiling mountain at Myanoshita. The dirty white deposit gave place to lime whiter than snow; and I found a basin which some learned hotel-keeper has christened Cleopatra's pitcher, or Mark

89

Antony's whisky-jug, or something equally poetical. It was made of frosted silver; it was filled with water as clear as the sky. I do not know the depth of that wonder. The eye looked down beyond grottoes and caves of beryl into an abyss that communicated directly with the central fires of earth. And the pool was in pain, so that it could not refrain from talking about it; muttering and chattering and moaning. From the lips of the lime-ledges, forty feet under water, spurts of silver bubbles would fly up and break the peace of the crystal atop. Then the whole pool would shake and grow dim, and there were noises. I removed myself only to find other pools all equally unhappy, rifts in the ground, full of running, red-hot water, slippery sheets of deposit overlaid with greenish gray hot water, and here and there pit-holes dry as a rifled tomb in India, dusty and waterless. Elsewhere the infernal waters had first boiled dead and then embalmed the pines and underwood, or the forest trees had taken heart and smothered up a blind formation with greenery, so that it was only by scraping the earth you could tell what fires had raged beneath. Yet the pines will win the battle in years to come, because Nature, who first forges all her work in her great smithies, has nearly finished this job, and is ready to temper it in the soft brown earth. The fires are dying down; the hotel is built where terraces have overflowed into flat wastes of deposits; the pines have taken possession of the high ground whence the terraces first started. Only the actual curve of the cataract stands clear, and it is guarded by soldiers who patrol it with loaded six-shooters, in order that the tourist may not bring up fence-rails and sink them in a pool, or chip the fretted tracery of the formations with a geological hammer, or, walking where the crust is too thin, foolishly cook himself.

I maneuvered round those soldiers. They were cavalry in a very slovenly uniform, dark-blue blouse, and light-blue trousers unstrapped, cut spoon-shape over the boot; cartridge belt, revolver, peaked cap, and worsted gloves—black buttons! By the mercy of Allah I opened conversation with a spectacled Scot. He had served the Queen in the Marines and a Line regiment, and the "go-fever" being in his bones, had drifted to America, there to serve Uncle

Sam. We sat on the edge of an extinct little pool, that under happier circumstances would have grown into a geyser, and began to discuss things generally. To us appeared yet another soldier. No need to ask his nationality or to be told that the troop called him "The Henglishman." A cockney was he, who had seen something of warfare in Egypt, and had taken his discharge from a Fusilier regiment not unknown to you.

"And how do things go?"

"Very much as you please," said they. "There's not half the discipline here that there is in the Queen's service—not half—nor the work either, but what there is, is rough work. Why, there's a sergeant now with a black eye that one of our men gave him. They won't say anything about that, of course. Our punishments? Fines mostly, and then if you carry on too much you go to the cooler—that's the clink. Yes, Sir. Horses? Oh, they're devils, these Montana horses. Bronchos mostly. We don't slick 'em up for parade—not much. And the amount of schooling that you put into one English troop-horse would be enough for a whole squadron of these creatures. You'll meet more troopers further up the Park. Go and look at their horses and their turnouts. I fancy it'll startle you. I'm wearing a made tie and a breastpin under my blouse? Of course I am! I can wear anything I darn please. We aren't particular here. I shouldn't dare come on parade—no, nor yet fatigue duty—in this condition in the Old Country; but it don't matter here. But don't you forget, Sir, that it's taught me how to trust to myself, and my shooting irons. I don't want fifty orders to move across the Park, and catch a poacher. Yes, they poach here. Men come in with an outfit and ponies, smuggle in a gun or two, and shoot the bison. If you interfere, they shoot at you. Then you confiscate all their outfit and their ponies. We have a pond full of them now down below. There's our Captain over yonder. Speak to him if you want to know anything special. This service isn't a patch on the Old Country's service; but you look, if it was worked up it would be just a Hell of a service. But these citizens despise us, and they put us on to road-mending, and such like. 'Nough to ruin an army."

To the Captain I addressed myself after my friends had gone.

They told me that a good many American officers dressed by the French army. The Captain certainly might have been mistaken for a French officer of light cavalry, and he had more than the courtesy of a Frenchman. Yes, he had read a good deal about our Indian warfare, and had been much struck with the likeness it bore to Red Indian warfare. I had better, when I reached the next cavalry post, scattered between two big geyser basins, introduce myself to a Captain and Lieutenant. They could show me things. He himself was devoting all his time to conserving the terraces, and surreptitiously running hot water into dried-up basins that fresh pools might form. "I get very interested in that sort of thing. It's not duty, but it's what I'm put here for." And then he began to talk of his troop as I have heard his brethren in India talk. Such a troop! Built up carefully, and watched lovingly; "not a man that I'd wish to exchange, and, what's more, I believe not a man that would wish to leave on his own account. We're different, I believe, from the English. Your officers value the horses; we set store on the men. We train them more than we do the horses."

Of the American trooper I will tell you more hereafter. He is not a gentleman to be trifled with.

Next dawning, entering a buggy of fragile construction, with the old people from Chicago, I embarked on my perilous career. We ran straight up a mountain till we could see, sixty miles away, the white houses of Cook City on another mountain, and the whiplash-like trail leading thereto. The live air made me drunk. If Tom, the driver, had proposed to send the mares in a bee-line to the city, I should have assented, and so would the old lady, who chewed gum and talked about her symptoms. The tub-ended rock-dog, which is but the translated prairie-dog, broke across the road under our horses' feet, the rabbit and the chipmunk danced with fright; we heard the roar of the river, and the road went round a corner. On one side piled rock and shale, that enjoined silence for fear of a general slide-down; on the other a sheer drop, and a fool of a noisy river below. Then, apparently in the middle of the road, lest any should find driving too easy, a post of rock. Nothing beyond that save the flank of a cliff. Then my stomach departed from me, as it does when you swing, for we left the dirt, which was at least some guarantee of safety, and sailed round the curve, and up a steep incline, on a plank-road built out from the cliff. The planks were nailed at the outer edge, and did not shift or creak very much—but enough, quite enough. That was the Golden Gate. I got my stomach back again when we trotted out on to a vast upland adorned with a lake and hills. Have you ever seen an untouched land—the face of virgin Nature? It is rather a curious sight, because the hills are choked with timber that has never known an ax, and the storm has rent a way through this timber, so that a hundred thousand trees lie matted together in swathes; and, since each tree lies where it falls, you may behold trunk and branch returning to the earth whence they sprang—exactly as the body of man returns—each limb making its own little grave, the grass climbing above the bark, till at last there remains only the outline of a tree upon the rank undergrowth.

Then we drove under a cliff of obsidian, which is black glass, some two hundred feet high; and the road at its foot was made of black glass that crackled. This was no great matter, because half an hour before, Tom had pulled up in the woods that we might sufficiently admire a mountain who stood all by himself, shaking with laughter or rage.

The glass cliff overlooks a lake where the beavers built a dam about a mile and a half long in a zig-zag line, as their necessities prompted. Then came the Government and strictly preserved them, and, as you shall learn later on, they be damn impudent beasts. The old lady had hardly explained the natural history of beavers before we climbed some hills—it really didn't matter in that climate, because we could have scaled the stars—and (this mattered very much indeed) shot down a desperate, dusky slope, brakes shrieking on the wheels, the mares clicking among unseen rocks, the dust dense as a fog, and a wall of trees on either side. "How do the heavy four-horse coaches take it, Tom?" I asked, remembering that some twenty-three souls had gone that way half an hour before. "Take it at the run!" said Tom, spitting out the dust. Of course there was a sharp curve, and a bridge at the bottom, but luckily nothing met us, and we came to a wooden shanty called a hotel, in time for a crazy tiffin served by very gorgeous handmaids with very pink cheeks. When health fails in other and more exciting pursuits, a season as "help" in one of the Yellowstone hotels will restore the frailest constitution.

Then by companies after tiffin we walked chattering to the uplands of Hell. They call it the Norris Geyser Basin on Earth. It was as though the tide of desolation had gone out, but would presently return, across innumerable acres of dazzling white geyser formation. There were no terraces here, but all other horrors. Not ten yards from the road a blast of steam shot up roaring every few seconds, a mud volcano spat filth to Heaven, streams of hot water rumbled under foot, plunged through the dead pines in steaming cataracts and died on a waste of white where green-gray, black-yellow, and linked pools roared, shouted, bubbled, or hissed as their wicked fancies prompted. By the look of the eye the place should have been frozen over. By the feel of the feet it was warm. I ventured out among the pools, carefully following tracks, but one unwary foot began to sink, a squirt of water followed, and having no desire to descend quick into Tophet I returned to the shore where the mud and the sulphur and the nameless fat ooze-vegetation of Lethe lay. But the very road rang as though built over a gulf; and besides, how was I to tell when the raving blast of steam would find its vent insufficient and blow the whole affair into Nirvana? There was a potent stench of stale eggs everywhere, and crystals of sulphur crumbled under the foot, and the glare of the sun on the white stuff was blinding. Sitting under a bank, to me appeared a young trooper—ex-Cape mounted Rifles, this man: the real American seems to object to his army—mounted on a horse half-maddened by the noise and steam and smell. He carried only the six-shooter and cartridge-belt. On service the Springfield carbine (which is clumsy) and a cartridge-belt slung diagonally complete equipment. The sword is no earthly use for Border warfare and, except at state parades, is never worn. The saddle is the McClellan tree over a four-folded blanket. Sweat-leathers you must pay for yourself. And the beauty of the tree is that it necessitates first very careful girthing and a thorough knowledge of tricks with the blanket to suit the varying conditions of the horse—a broncho will bloat in a night if he can get a bellyful—

and, secondly, even more careful riding to prevent galling. Crup-
per and breast-band do seem to be used,—but they are casual
about their accouterments,—and the bit is the single, jaw-break-
ing curb which American war-pictures show us. That young man
was very handsome, and the gray service hat—most like the under
half of a seedy terai—shaded his strong face admirably as his
horse backed and shivered and sidled and plunged all over the
road, and he lectured from his saddle, one foot out of the heavy-
hooded stirrup, one hand on the sweating neck. "He's not used to
the Park, this brute, and he's a confirmed bolter on parade; but
we understand each other." *Whoosh!* went the steam-blast down
the road with a dry roar. Round spun the troop horse prepared to
bolt, and, his momentum being suddenly checked, reared till I
thought he would fall back on his rider. "Oh, no; we settled that
little matter when I was breaking him," said Centaur. "He used
to try to fall back on me. Isn't he a devil? I think you'd laugh to
see the way our regiments are horsed. Sometimes a big Montana
beast like mine has a thirteen-two broncho pony for a neighbor,
and it's annoying if you're used to better things. And oh, how you
have to ride your mount! It's necessary; but I can tell you at the
end of a long day's march, when you'd give all the world to ride
like a sack, it isn't sweet to get extra drill for slouching. When
we're turned out, we're turned out for *anything*—not a fifteen-mile
trot, but for the use and behoof of all the Northern States. I've
been in Arizona. A trooper there who had been in India told me
that Arizona was like Afghanistan. There's nothing under Heaven
there except horned toads and rattlesnakes—and Indians. Our
trouble is that we only deal with Indians and they don't teach us
much, and of course the citizens look down on us and all that. As a
matter of fact, I suppose we're really only mounted infantry, but
remember we're the best mounted infantry in the world." And the
horse danced a fandango in proof.

"My faith!" said I, looking at the dusty blouse, gray hat, soiled
leather accouterments, and whalebone poise of the wearer. "If
they are all like you, you are."

"Thanks, whoever you may be. Of course if we were turned into
a lawn-tennis court and told to resist, say, your heavy cavalry,

we'd be ridden off the face of the earth if we couldn't get away. We have neither the weight nor the drill for a charge. My horse, for instance, by English standards, is half-broken, and like all the others, he bolts when we're in line. But cavalry charge against cavalry charge doesn't happen often, and if it did, well—all our men know that up to a hundred yards they are absolutely safe behind this old thing." He patted his revolver pouch. "Absolutely safe from any shooting of yours. What man do you think would dare to use a pistol at even thirty yards, if his life depended on it? Not one of *your* men. They can't shoot. We can. You'll hear about that down the Park—further up."

Then he added, courteously: "Just now it seems that the English supply all the men to the American Army. That's what makes them so good perhaps." And with mutual expressions of good-will we parted—he to an outlying patrol fifteen miles away, I to my buggy and the old lady, who, regarding the horrors of the fire-holes, could only say, "Good Lord!" at thirty-second intervals. Her husband talked about "dreffel waste of steam-power," and we went on in the clear, crisp afternoon, speculating as to the formation of geysers.

"What I say," shrieked the old lady *apropos* of matters theological, "and what I say more, after having seen all that, is that the Lord has ordained a Hell for such as disbelieve His gracious works."

Nota bene.—Tom had profanely cursed the near mare for stumbling. He looked straight in front of him and said no word, but the left corner of his left eye flickered in my direction.

"And if," continued the old lady, "if we find a thing so dreffel as all that steam and sulphur allowed on the face of the earth, mustn't we believe that there is something ten thousand times more terrible below prepared un*toe* our destruction?"

Some people have a wonderful knack of extracting comfort from things. I am ashamed to say I agreed ostentatiously with the old lady. She developed the personal view of the matter.

"*Now* I shall be able to say something to Anna Fincher about her way of living. Shan't I, Blake?" This to her husband.

"Yes," said he, speaking slowly after a heavy tiffin. "But the girl's a good girl;" and they fell to arguing as to whether the luckless Anna Fincher really stood in need of lectures edged with Hell fire (she went to dances, I believe), while I got out and walked in the dust alongside of Tom.

"I drive blame cur'ous kinder folk through this place," said he. "Blame cur'ous. 'Seems a pity that they should ha' come so far just to liken Norris Basin to Hell. 'Guess Chicago would ha' served 'em, speaking in comparison, jest as good."

We curved the hill and entered a forest of spruce, the path serpentining between the tree-boles, the wheels running silent on immemorial mold. There was nothing alive in the forest save ourselves. Only a river was speaking angrily somewhere to the right. For miles we drove till Tom bade us alight and look at certain falls. Wherefore we stepped out of that forest and nearly fell down a cliff which guarded a tumbled river and returned demanding fresh miracles. If the water had run up-hill, we should perhaps have taken more notice of it; but 'twas only a waterfall, and I really forget whether the water was warm or cold. There is a stream here called Firehole River. It is fed by the overflow from the various geysers and basins,—a warm and deadly river wherein no fish breed. I think we crossed it a few dozen times in the course of a day.

Then the sun began to sink, and there was a taste of frost about, and we went swiftly from the forest into the open, dashed across a branch of the Firehole River and found a wood shanty, even rougher than the last at which, after a forty-mile drive, we were to dine and sleep. Half a mile from this place stood, on the banks of the Firehole River, a "beaver-lodge," and there were rumors of bears and other cheerful monsters in the woods on the hill at the back of the building.

In the cool, crisp quiet of the evening I sought that river, and found a pile of newly gnawed sticks and twigs. The beaver works with the cold-chisel, and a few clean strokes suffice to level a four-inch bole. Across the water on the far bank glimmered, with the ghastly white of peeled dead timber, the beaver-lodge—a mass of disheveled branches. The inhabitants had dammed the stream lower down and spread it into a nice little lake. The question was would they come out for their walk before it got too dark to see.

They came—blessings on their blunt muzzles, they came—as shadows come, drifting down the stream, stirring neither foot nor tail. There were three of them. One went down to investigate the state of the dam; the other two began to look for supper. There is only one thing more startling than the noiselessness of a tiger in the jungle, and that is the noiselessness of a beaver in the water. The straining ear could catch no sound whatever till they began to eat the thick green river-scudge that they call beaver-grass. I, bowed among the logs, held my breath and stared with all my eyes. They were not ten yards from me, and they would have eaten their dinner in peace so long as I had kept absolutely still. They were dear and desirable beasts, and I was just preparing to creep a step nearer when that wicked old lady from Chicago clattered down the bank, an umbrella in her hand, shrieking: "Beavers, beavers! Young man, whurr are those beavers? Good Lord! What was that now?"

The solitary watcher might have heard a pistol shot ring through the air. I wish it had killed the old lady, but it was only the beaver giving warning of danger with the slap of his tail on the water. It was exactly like the "phink" of a pistol fired with damp powder. Then there were no more beavers—not a whisker-end. The lodge, however, was there, and a beast lower than any beaver began to throw stones at it because the old lady from Chicago said: "P'raps, if you rattle them up they'll come out. I do so want to see a beaver."

Yet it cheers me to think I have seen the beaver in his wilds. Never will I go to the Zoo. That evening, after supper—'twere flattery to call it dinner—a Captain and a Subaltern of the cavalry post appeared at the hotel. These were the officers of whom the Mammoth Springs Captain had spoken. The Lieutenant had read everything that he could lay hands on about the Indian army, especially our cavalry arrangements, and was very full of a scheme for raising the riding Red Indians—it is not every noble savage that will make a trooper—into frontier levies—a sort of Khyber guard.[1] "Only," as he said ruefully, "there is no frontier these

---

[1] The *Khyber Guard* was a special defensive force created by the British to protect the Khyber Pass on the border of West Pakistan and Afghanistan. The pass was the primary entry into India from the Northwest and the principal route for armies invading India, including those of Alexander the Great.

days, and all our Indian wars are nearly over. Those beautiful beasts will die out, and nobody will ever know what splendid cavalry they can make."

The Captain told stories of Border warfare—of ambush, firing on the rear-guard, heat that split the skull better than any tomahawk, cold that wrinkled the very liver, night-stampedes of baggage-mules, raiding of cattle, and hopeless stern-chases into inhospitable hills, when the cavalry knew that they were not only being outpaced but outspied. Then he spoke of one fair charge when a tribe gave battle in the open and the troopers rode in swordless, firing right and left with their revolvers and—it was excessively uncomfy for that tribe. And I spoke of what men had told me of huntings in Burma, of hill-climbing in the Black Mountain affair, and so forth.

"Exactly!" said the Captain. "Nobody knows and nobody cares. What does it matter to the Down-Easter who Wrap-up-his-Tail was?"

"And what does the fat Briton know or care about Boh Hla-Oo?" said I. Then both together: "Depend upon it, my dear, Sir, the army in both Anglo-Saxon countries is a mischievously underestimated institution, and it's a pleasure to meet a man who," etc., etc. And we nodded triangularly in all good will, and swore eternal friendship. The Lieutenant made a statement which rather amazed me. He said that, on account of the scarcity of business, many American officers were to be found getting practical instruction from little troubles among the South American Republics. When the need broke out they would return. "There is so little for us to do, and the Republic has a trick of making us hedge and ditch for our pay. A little road-making on service is not a bad thing, but continuous navvying is enough to knock the heart out of any army."

I agreed, and we sat up till two in the morning swapping the lies of East and West. As that glorious Chief Man-afraid-of-Pink-Rats once said to the Agent on the Reservation: "'Melican officer good man. Heap good man. Drink me. Drink he. Drink me. Drink he. Drink *he*. Me blind. *Heap* good man!"

X

"What man would read and read the selfsame faces
And like the marbles which the windmill grinds,
Rub smooth forever with the same smooth minds,
This year retracing last year's every year's dull traces,
Where there are woods and unmanstifled places?"

— *Lowell.*

Once upon a time there was a carter who brought his team and a friend into the Yellowstone Park without due thought. Presently they came upon a few of the natural beauties of the place, and that carter turned his team into his friend's team howling: "Get back o' this, Jim. All Hell's alight under our noses." And they call the place Hell's Half-acre to this day. We, too, the old lady from Chicago, her husband, Tom, and the good little mares came to Hell's Half-acre, which is about sixty acres, and when Tom said: "Would you like to drive over it?" we said: "Certainly no, and if you do, we shall report you to the authorities." There was a plain, blistered and peeled and abominable, and it was given over to the sportings and spoutings of devils who threw mud and steam and dirt at each other with whoops and halloos and bellowing curses. The place smelt of the refuse of the Pit, and that odor mixed with the clean, wholesome aroma of the pines in our nostrils throughout the day. Be it known that the Park is laid out, like Ollendorf, in exercises of progressive difficulty. Hell's Half-acre was a prelude to ten or twelve miles of geyser formation. We passed hot streams boiling in the forest; saw whiffs of steam beyond these, and yet other whiffs breaking through the misty green hills in the far distance; we trampled on sulphur, and sniffed things much worse than any sulphur which is known to the upper world; and so came upon a parklike place where Tom suggested we should get out and play with the geysers.

Imagine mighty green fields splattered with lime beds: all the flowers of the summer growing up to the very edge of the lime. That was the first glimpse of the geyser basins. The buggy had pulled up close to a rough, broken, blistered cone of stuff between ten and twenty feet high. There was trouble in that place —moaning, splashing, gurgling and the clank of machinery. A spurt of boiling water jumped into the air and a wash of water followed. I removed swiftly. The old lady from Chicago shrieked. "What a wicked waste!" said her husband. I think they call it the Riverside Geyser. Its spout was torn and ragged like the mouth of a gun when a shell has burst there. It grumbled madly for a moment or two and then was still. I crept over the steaming lime—it was the burning marl on which Satan lay—and looked fearfully down its mouth. You should never look a gift geyser in the mouth. I beheld a horrible slippery slimy funnel with water rising and falling ten feet at a time. Then the water rose to lip level with a rush and an infernal bubbling troubled this Devil's Bethesda before the sullen heave of the crest of a wave lapped over the edge and made me run. Mark the nature of the human soul! I had begun with awe, not to say terror. I stepped back from the flanks of the Riverside Geyser saying: "Pooh! Is that all it can do?" Yet for aught I knew the whole thing might have blown up at a minute's notice; she, he, or it being an arrangement of uncertain temper.

We drifted on up that miraculous valley. On either side of us were hills from a thousand to fifteen hundred feet high and wooded from heel to crest. As far as the eye could range forward were columns of steam in the air, misshapen lumps of lime, most like preadamite monsters, still pools of turquoise blue, stretches of blue corn-flowers, a river that coiled on itself twenty times, bowlders of strange colors, and ridges of glaring, staring white.

The old lady from Chicago poked with her parasol at the pools as though they had been alive. On one particularly innocent-looking little puddle she turned her back for a moment, and there rose behind her a twenty-foot column of water and steam. Then she shrieked and protested that "she never thought it would ha' done it," and the old man chewed his tobacco steadily, and mourned for steam power wasted. I embraced the whitened stump of a middle-sized pine that had grown all too close to a hot pool's lip, and the whole thing turned over under my hand as a tree would do in a nightmare. From right and left came the trumpetings of elephants at play. I stepped into a pool of old dried blood rimmed with the nodding cornflowers; and the blood changed to ink even as I trod! and ink and blood were washed away in a spurt of boiling sulphurous water spat out from the lee of a bank of flowers. This sounds mad, doesn't it?

A moonfaced trooper of German extraction—never was Park so carefully patrolled—came up to inform us that as yet we had not seen any of the real geysers, that they were all a mile or so up the valley, tastefully scattered round the hotel in which we would rest for the night. America is a free country, but the citizens look down on the soldier. *I* had to entertain that trooper. The old lady from Chicago would have none of him; so we loafed along together, now across half-rotten pine logs sunk in the swampy ground, anon over the ringing geyser formation, then knee-deep through long grass.

"And why did you 'list?" said I.

The moonfaced one's face began to work. I thought he would have a fit, but he told me a story instead—such a nice tale of a naughty little girl who wrote love letters to two men at once. She was a simple village wife, but a wicked "Family Novelette" countess couldn't have accomplished her ends better. She drove one man nearly wild with her pretty little treachery; and the other man abandoned her and came West to forget. Moonface was that man. We rounded a low spur of hill, and came out upon a field of aching snowy lime, rolled in sheets, twisted into knots, riven with rents and diamonds and stars, stretching for more than half a mile in every direction. In this place of despair lay most of the big geysers who know when there is trouble in Krakatoa, who tell the pines when there is a cyclone on the Atlantic seaboard, and who—are exhibited to visitors under pretty and fanciful names. The first mound that I encountered belonged to a goblin splashing in his tub. I heard him kick, pull a shower-bath on his shoulders, gasp, crack his joints, and rub himself down with a towel; then he let the water out of the bath, as a thoughtful man should, and it all sank down out of sight till another goblin arrived. Yet they called this place the Lioness and the Cubs. It lies not very far from the Lion, which is a sullen, roaring beast, and they say when it is very active the other geysers presently follow suit. After the Krakatoa eruption all the geysers went mad together, spouting, spurting, and bellowing till men feared that they would rip up the whole field. Mysterious sympathies exist among them, and when the Giantess speaks (of her more anon) they all hold their peace.

I was watching a solitary spring, when, far across the fields, stood up a plume of spun glass, iridescent and superb, against the sky. "That," said the trooper, "is Old Faithful. He goes off every sixty-five minutes to the minute, plays for five minutes, and sends up a column of water a hundred and fifty feet high. By the time you have looked at all the other geysers he will be ready to play."

So we looked and we wondered at the Beehive, whose mouth is built up exactly like a hive; at the Turban (which is not in the least like a turban); and at many, many other geysers, hot holes, and springs. Some of them rumbled, some hissed, some went off spasmodically, and others lay still in sheets of sapphire and beryl.

Would you believe that even these terrible creatures have to be guarded by the troopers to prevent the irreverent American from chipping the cones to pieces, or worse still, making the geysers sick? If you take of soft-soap a small barrelful and drop it down a geyser's mouth, the geyser will presently be forced to lay all before you and for days afterwards will be of an irritated and inconsistent stomach. When they told me the tale I was filled with sympathy. Now I wish that I had stolen soap and tried the experiment on some lonely little beast of a geyser in the woods. It sounds so probable—and so human.

Yet he would be a bold man who would administer emetics to the Giantess. She is flat-lipped, having no mouth, she looks like a pool, fifty feet long and thirty wide, and there is no ornamentation about her. At irregular intervals she speaks, and sends

103

up a column of water over two hundred feet high to begin with; then she is angry for a day and a half—sometimes for two days. Owing to her peculiarity of going mad in the night not many people have seen the Giantess at her finest; but the clamor of her unrest, men say, shakes the wooden hotel, and echoes like thunder among the hills. When I saw her trouble was brewing. The pool bubbled seriously, and at five-minute intervals, sank a foot or two, then rose, washed over the rim, and huge steam bubbles broke on the top. Just before an eruption the water entirely disappears from view. Whenever you see the water die down in a geyser-mouth get away as fast as you can. I saw a tiny little geyser suck in its breath in this way, and instinct made me retire while it hooted after me.

Leaving the Giantess to swear, and spit, and thresh about, we went over to Old Faithful, who by reason of his faithfulness has benches close to him whence you may comfortably watch. At the appointed hour we heard the water flying up and down the mouth with the sob of waves in a cave. Then came the preliminary gouts, then a roar and a rush, and that glittering column of diamonds rose, quivered, stood still for a minute. Then it broke, and the rest was a confused snarl of water not thirty feet high. All the young ladies—not more than twenty—in the tourist band remarked that it was "elegant," and betook themselves to writing their names in the bottoms of shallow pools. Nature fixes the insult indelibly, and the after-years will learn that "Hattie," "Sadie," "Mamie," "Sophie," and so forth, have taken out their hairpins, and scrawled in the face of Old Faithful.

The congregation returned to the hotel to put down their impressions in diaries and notebooks which they wrote up ostentatiously in the verandas. It was a sweltering hot day, albeit we stood somewhat higher than the summit of Jakko, and I left that raw pine-creaking caravanserai for the cool shade of a clump of pine between whose trunks glimmered tents. A batch of troopers came down the road, and flung themselves across country into their rough lines. Verily the 'Melican cavalry-man *can* ride, though he keeps his accouterments pig, and his horse cow-fashion.

I was free of that camp in five minutes—free to play with the heavy lumpy carbines, to have the saddles stripped, and punch the horses knowingly in the ribs. One of the men had been in the fight with "Wrap-up-his-Tail" before alluded to, and he told me how that great chief, his horse's tail tied up in red calico, swaggered in front of the United States cavalry, challenging all to single combat. But he was slain, and a few of his tribe with him. "There's no use in an Indian, anyway," concluded my friend.

A couple of cowboys—real cowboys, not the Buffalo Bill article —jingled through the camp amid a shower of mild chaff. They were on their way to Cook City, I fancy, and I know that they never washed. But they were picturesque ruffians with long spurs, hooded stirrups, slouch hats, fur weather-cloths over their knees, and pistol-butts easy to hand.

"The cowboy's goin' under before long," said my friend. "Soon as the country's settled up he'll have to go. But he's mighty useful now. What should we do without the cowboy?"

"As how?" said I, and the camp laughed.

"He has the money. We have the know-how. He comes in in winter to play poker at the military posts. *We* play poker—a few. When he's lost his money we make him drunk and let him go. Sometimes we get the wrong man." And he told a tale of an innocent cowboy who turned up, cleaned out, at a post, and played poker for thirty-six hours. But it was the post that was cleaned out when that long-haired Caucasian Ah Sin removed himself, heavy with everybody's pay, and declining the proffered liquor. "Naow," said the historian, "I don't play with no cowboy unless he's a little bit drunk first."

Ere I departed I gathered from more than one man that significant fact that *up to one hundred yards* he felt absolutely secure behind his revolver.

"In England, I understand," quoth a limber youth from the South, "in England a man aren't allowed to play with no firearms. He's got to be taught all that when he enlists. I didn't want much teaching how to shoot straight 'fore I served Uncle Sam. And that's just where it is. But you was talking about your horse-guards now?"

I explained briefly some peculiarities of equipment connected with our crackest crack cavalry. I grieve to say the camp roared.

"Take 'em over swampy ground. Let 'em run around a bit an' work the starch out of 'em, an' then, Almighty, if we wouldn't plug 'em at ease I'd eat their horses!"

"But suppose they engaged in the open?" said I.

"Engage the Hades. Not if there was a tree-trunk within twenty miles they *couldn't* engage in the open!"

Gentlemen, the Officers, have you ever seriously considered the existence on earth of a cavalry who by preference would fight in timber? The evident sincerity of the proposition made me think hard as I moved over to the hotel and joined a party exploration, which, diving into the woods, unearthed a pit pool of burningest water fringed with jet black sand—all the ground near by being pure white. But miracles pall when they arrive at the rate of twenty a day. A flaming dragonfly flew over the pool, reeled and dropped on the water, dying without a quiver of his gorgeous wings, and the pool said nothing whatever, but sent its thin steam wreaths up to the burning sky. I prefer pools that talk.

There was a maiden—a very trim maiden—who had just stepped out of one of Mr. James's novels. She owned a delightful mother and an equally delightful father, a heavy-eyed, slow-voiced man of finance. The parents thought that their daughter wanted change. She lived in New Hampshire. Accordingly, she had dragged them up to Alaska, to the Yosemite Valley, and was now returning leisurely via the Yellowstone just in time for the tail-end of the summer season at Saratoga. We had met once or twice before in the Park, and I had been amazed and amused at her critical commendation of the wonders that she saw. From that very resolute little mouth I received a lecture on American literature, the nature and inwardness of Washington society, the precise value of Cable's works as compared with "Uncle Remus" Harris, and a few other things that had nothing whatever to do with geysers, but were altogether delightful. Now an English maiden who had stumbled on a dust-grimed, lime-washed, sun-peeled, collarless wanderer come from and going to goodness knows where, would, her mother inciting her and her father brandishing his umbrella, have regarded him as a dissolute adventurer. Not so those delightful people from New Hampshire. They were good enough to treat me—it sounds almost incredible—as a human being, possibly respectable, probably not in immediate need of financial assistance. Papa talked pleasantly and to the point. The little maiden strove valiantly with the accent of her birth and that of her reading, and mama smiled benignly in the background.

Balance this with a story of a young English idiot I met knocking about inside his high collars, attended by a valet. He condescended to tell me that "you can't be too careful who you talk to in these parts," and stalked on, fearing, I suppose, every minute for his social chastity. Now that man was a barbarian (I took occasion to tell him so), for he comported himself after the manner of the head-hunters of Assam, who are at perpetual feud one with another.

You will understand that these foolish tales are introduced in order to cover the fact that this pen cannot describe the glories of the Upper Geyser basin. The evening I spent under the lee of the Castle Geyser sitting on a log with some troopers and watching a baronial keep forty feet high spouting hot water. If the Castle went off first, they said the Giantess would be quiet, and *vice versa;* and then they told tales till the moon got up and a party of campers in the woods gave us all something to eat.

Next morning Tom drove us on, promising new wonders. He pulled up after a few miles at a clump of brushwood where an army was drowning. I could hear the sick gasps and thumps of men going under, but when I broke through the brushwood the hosts had fled, and there were only pools of pink, black, and white lime, thick as turbid honey. They shot up a pat of mud every minute or two, choking in the effort. It was an uncanny sight. Do you wonder that in the old days the Indians were careful to avoid the Yellowstone? Geysers are permissible, but mud is terrifying. The old lady from Chicago took a piece of it, and in half an hour it dried into lime-dust and blew away between her fingers. All *maya,*—illusion,—you see! Then we clinked over sulphur in crystals; there was a waterfall of boiling water; and a road across a level park hotly contested by the beavers. Every winter they build their dam and flood the low-lying land; every summer that dam is torn up by the Government, and for half a mile you must plow axle-deep in water, the willows brushing into the buggy, and little waterways branching off right and left. The road is the main stream—just like the Bolan line in flood. If you turn up a byway, there is no more of you, and the beavers work your buggy into next year's dam.

Then came soft, turfy forest that deadened the wheels, and two troopers—on detachment duty—came noiselessly behind us. One was the Wrap-up-his-Tail man, and we talked merrily while the half-broken horses bucked about among the trees till we came to a mighty hill all strewn with moss agates, and everybody had to get out and pant in that thin air. But how intoxicating it was! The old lady from Chicago clucked like an emancipated hen as she scuttled about the road cramming pieces of rock into her reticule. She sent me fifty yards down the hill to pick up a piece of broken bottle which she insisted was moss agate. "I've some o' that at home an' they shine. You go get it, young feller."

As we climbed the long path the road grew viler and viler till it became without disguise the bed of a torrent; and just when things were at their rockiest we emerged into a little sapphire lake—but never sapphire was so blue—called Mary's lake; and that between eight and nine thousand feet above the sea. Then came grass downs, all on a vehement slope, so that the buggy following the new-made road ran on to the two off-wheels mostly, till we dipped head-first into a ford, climbed up a cliff, raced along a down, dipped again and pulled up disheveled at "Larry's" for lunch and an hour's rest. Only "Larry" could have managed that school-feast tent on the lonely hillside. Need I say that he was an Irishman? His supplies were at their lowest ebb, but Larry enveloped us all in the golden glamor of his speech ere we had descended, and the tent with the rude trestle-table became a palace, the rough fare, delicacies of Delmonico, and we, the abashed recipients of Larry's imperial bounty. It was only later that I discovered I had paid eight shillings for tinned beef, biscuits, and beer, but on the other hand Larry had said: "Will I go out an' kill a buffalo?" And I felt that for me and for me alone would he have done it. Everybody else felt that way. Good luck go with Larry!

"An' now you'll all go an' wash your pocket-handkerchiefs in that beautiful hot spring round the corner," said he. "There's soap an' a washboard ready, an' 'tis not every day that ye can get hot water for nothing." He waved us large-handedly to the open downs while he put the tent to rights. There was no sense of fatigue on the body or distance in the air. Hill and dale rode on the eyeball. I could have clutched the far-off snowy peaks by putting out my hand. Never was such maddening air. Why we should have washed pocket-handkerchiefs Larry alone knows. It appeared to be a sort of religious rite. In a little valley overhung with gay painted rocks ran a stream of velvet brown and pink. It was hot—hotter than the hand could bear—and it colored the bowlders in its course.

There was the maiden from New Hampshire, the old lady from Chicago, papa, mama, the woman who chewed gum, and all the rest of them, gravely bending over a washboard and soap. Mysterious virtues lay in that queer stream. It turned the linen white as driven snow in five minutes, and then we lay on the grass and laughed with sheer bliss of being alive. This have I known once in Japan, once on the banks of the Columbia, what time the salmon came in and "California" howled, and once again in the Yellowstone by the light of the eyes of the maiden from New Hampshire. Four little pools lay at my elbow: one was of black water (tepid), one clear water (cold), one clear water (hot), one red water (boiling); my newly washed handkerchief covered them all. We marveled as children marvel.

"This evening we shall do the grand cañon of the Yellowstone?" said the maiden.

"Together?" said I; and she said yes.

The sun was sinking when we heard the roar of falling waters and came to a broad river along whose banks we ran. And then— oh, then! I might at a pinch describe the infernal regions, but not the other place. Be it known to you that the Yellowstone River has occasion to run through a gorge about eight miles long. To get to the bottom of the gorge it makes two leaps, one of about one hundred and twenty and the other of three hundred feet. I investigated the upper or lesser fall, which is close to the hotel. Up to that time nothing particular happens to the Yellowstone, its banks being only rocky, rather steep, and plentifully adorned with pines. At the falls it comes round a corner, green, solid, ribbed with a little foam not more than thirty yards wide. Then it goes over still green and rather more solid than before. After a minute or two you, sitting upon a rock directly above the drop, begin to understand that something has occurred; that the river has jumped a huge distance between solid cliff walls—and what looks like the gentle froth of ripples lapping the sides of the gorge below is really the outcome of great waves. And the river yells aloud; but the cliffs do not allow the yells to escape.

That inspection began with curiosity and finished in terror, for it seemed that the whole world was sliding in chrysolite from under my feet. I followed with the others round the corner to arrive at the brink of the cañon: we had to climb up a nearly perpendicular ascent to begin with, for the ground rises more than the river drops. Stately pine woods fringe either lip of the gorge, which is—the Gorge of the Yellowstone.

All I can say is that without warning or preparation I looked into a gulf seventeen hundred feet deep with eagles and fish-hawks circling far below. And the sides of that gulf were one wild welter of color—crimson, emerald, cobalt, ochre, amber, honey splashed with port-wine, snow-white, vermilion, lemon, and silver-gray, in wide washes. The sides did not fall sheer, but were graven by time and water and air into monstrous heads of kings, dead chiefs, men and women of the old time. So far below that no sound of its strife could reach us, the Yellowstone River ran—a finger-wide strip of jade-green. The sunlight took those wondrous walls and gave fresh hues to those that nature had already laid there. Once I saw the dawn break over a lake in Rajputana and the sun set over the Oodey Sagar amid a circle of Holman hills. This time I was watching both performances going on below me—upside down you understand—and the colors were real! The cañon was burning like Troy town; but it would burn forever, and, thank goodness, neither pen nor brush could ever portray its splendors adequately. The Academy would reject the picture for a chromolithograph. The public would scoff at the letter-press for Daily Telegraphese. "I will leave this thing alone," said I; "'tis my peculiar property. Nobody else shall share it with me." Evening crept through the pines that shadowed us, but the full glory of the day flamed in that cañon as we went out very cautiously to a jutting piece of rock—blood-red or pink it was—that overhung the deepest deeps of all. Now I know what it is to sit enthroned amid the clouds of sunset. Giddiness took away all sensation of touch or form; but the sense of blinding color remained. When I reached the mainland again I had sworn that I had been floating. The maid from New Hampshire said no word for a very long time. She then quoted poetry, which was perhaps the best thing she could have done.

"And to think that this show-place has been going on all these days an' none of we ever saw it," said the old lady from Chicago, with an acid glance at her husband.

"No, only the Injuns," said he, unmoved; and the maiden and I laughed long. Inspiration is fleeting, beauty is vain, and the power of the mind for wonder limited. Though the shining hosts themselves had risen choiring from the bottom of the gorge they would not have prevented her papa and one baser than himself from rolling stones down those stupendous rainbow-washed slides. Seventeen hundred feet of steepest pitch and rather more than seventeen hundred colors for log or boulder to whirl through! So we heaved things and saw them gather way and bound from white rock to red or yellow, dragging behind them torrents of color, till the noise of their descent ceased and they bounded a hundred yards clear at the last into the Yellowstone.

"I've been down there," said Tom that evening. "It's easy to get down if you're careful—just sit and slide; but getting up is worse. An' I found, down below there, two rocks just marked with a picture of the cañon. I wouldn't sell those rocks not for fifteen dollars."

And papa and I crawled down to the Yellowstone—just above the first little fall—to wet a line for good luck. The round moon came up and turned the cliffs and pines into silver; a two-pound trout came up also, and we slew him among the rocks, nearly tumbling into that wild river.

*

Then out and away to Livingston once more. The maiden from New Hampshire disappeared; papa and mama with her disappeared. Disappeared, too, the old lady from Chicago and all the rest, while I thought of all that I had *not* seen—the forest of petrified trees with amethyst crystals in their black hearts; the great Yellowstone Lake where you catch your trout alive in one spring and drop him into another to boil him; and most of all that mysterious Hoodoo region where all the devils not employed in the geysers live and kill the wandering bear and elk, so that the scared hunter finds in Death Gulch piled carcasses of the dead whom no man has smitten. Hoodoo-land with the overhead noises, the bird and beast and devil rocks, the mazes and the bottomless pits,—all these things I missed. On the return road Yankee Jim and Diana of the Crossways gave me kindly greeting as the train paused an instant before their door, and at Livingston whom should I see but Tom the driver?

"I've done with Yellowstone and decided to clear out East somewheres," said he. "Your talkin' about movin' round so gay an' careless made me kinder restless; I'm movin' out."

Lord forgive us for our responsibility one to another!

"And your partner?" said I.

"Here's him," said Tom, introducing a gawky youth with a bundle; and I saw those two young men turn their faces to the East.

XI

"A fool also is full of words:
a man cannot tell what shall be;
and what shall be after him who can tell?"

It has just occurred to me with great force that delightful as these letters are to myself their length and breadth and depth may be just the least little bit in the world wearisome to you over there. I will compress myself rigorously, though I should very much like to deliver a dissertation on the American Army and the possibilities of its extension.

The American Army is a beautiful little army. Some day, when all the Indians are happily dead or drunk, it ought to make the finest scientific and survey corps that the world has ever seen. It does excellent work now, but there is this defect in its nature; it is officered, as you know, from West Point, but the mischief of it is that West Point seems to be created for the purpose of spreading a general knowledge of military matters among the people. A boy goes up to that institution, gets his pass, and returns to civil life, so they tell me, with a dangerous knowledge that he is a sucking Moltke, and may apply his learning when occasion offers.[1] Given trouble, that man will be a nuisance, because he is a hideously versatile American to begin with, as cocksure of himself as a man can be, and with all the racial disregard for human life to back him through his demi-semi-professional generalship.

In a country where, as the records of the daily papers show, men engaged in a conflict with police or jails are all too ready to adopt a military formation, and get heavily shot in a sort of cheap, half-instructed warfare instead of being decently scared

[1]Helmuth von Moltke (1800-89), Prussian field marshal, writer on military affairs, and internationally prominent military strategist and tactician.

by the appearance of the military, this sort of arrangement does not seem wise.

The bond between the States is of amazing tenuity. So long as they do not absolutely march into the District of Columbia, sit on the Washington statue, and invent a flag of their own, they can legislate, lynch, hunt negroes through swamps, divorce, railroad, and rampage as much as ever they choose. They do not need knowledge of their own military strength to back their genial lawlessness.

That Regular Army, which is a dear little army, should be kept to itself, blooded on detachment duty, turned into the paths of science, and now and again assembled at feasts of Freemasons and so forth.

It's too tiny to be a political power. The immortal wreck of the Grand Army of the Republic is a political power of the largest and most unblushing description.

It ought not to help to lay the foundations of an amateur military power that is blind and irresponsible. . . .

Be thankful that the balance of this lecture is suppressed, and with it the account of a "shiveree" which I attended in Livingston City: and the story of the editor and the sub-editor (the latter was a pet cougar, or mountain lion, who used, they said, skillfully to sub-edit disputants in the office) of the Livingston daily paper.

Omitting a thousand matters of first importance, let me pick up the thread of things on a narrow-gauge line that took me down to Salt Lake. The run between Delhi and Ahmedabad on a May day would have been bliss compared to this torture. There was nothing but glare and desert and alkali dust. There was no smoking-accommodation. I sat in the lavatory with the conductor and a prospector who told stories about Indian atrocities in the voice of a dreaming child—oath following oath as smoothly as clotted cream laps the mouth of the jug. I don't think he knew he was saying anything out of the way, but nine or ten of those oaths were new to me, and one even made the conductor raise his eyebrows.

"And when a man's alone mostly, leadin' his horse across the hills, he gets to talk aloud to himself as it was," said the weatherworn retailer of tortures. A vision rose before me of this man tramping the Bannack City trail under the stars—swearing, always swearing.

Bundles of rags that were pointed out as Red Indians, boarded the train from time to time. Their race privileges allow them free transit on the platforms of the cars. They mustn't come inside of course, and equally of course the train never thinks of pulling up for them. I saw a squaw take us flying and leave us in the same manner when we were spinning round a curve. Like the Punjabi, the Red Indian gets out by preference on the trackless plain and walks stolidly to the horizon. He never says where he is going. . . .

Salt Lake. I am concerned for the sake of Mr. Phil Robinson, his soul. You will remember that he wrote a book called *Saints and Sinners* in which he proved very prettily that the Mormon was almost altogether an estimable person. Ever since my arrival at Salt Lake I have been wondering what made him write that book. On mature reflection, and after a long walk round the city, I am inclined to think it was the sun, which is very powerful hereabouts.

By great good luck the evil-minded train already delayed twelve hours by a burnt bridge, brought me to the city on a Saturday by way of that valley which the Mormons aver their efforts had caused to blossom like the rose. Some hours previously I had entered a new world where, in conversation, every one was either a Mormon or a Gentile. It is not seemly for a free and independent citizen to dub himself a Gentile, but the Mayor of Ogden—which is the Gentile city of the valley—told me that there must be some distinction between the two flocks.

Long before the fruit orchards of Logan or the shining levels of the Salt Lake had been reached that Mayor—himself a Gentile, and one renowned for his dealings with the Mormons—told me that the great question of the existence of the power within the power was being gradually solved by the ballot and by education.

"We have," quoth he, "hills round and about here, stuffed full of silver and gold and lead, and all Hell atop of the Mormon church can't keep the Gentile from flocking in when that's the case. At Ogden, thirty miles from Salt Lake, this year the Gentile vote swamped the Mormon at the Municipal elections, and next year we trust that we shall be able to repeat our success in Salt Lake itself. In that city the Gentiles are only one-third of the total population, but the mass of 'em are grown men, capable of voting. Whereas the Mormons are cluttered up with children. I guess as soon as we have purely Gentile officers in the township, and the control of the policy of the city, the Mormons will have to back down considerable. They're bound to go before long. My own notion is that it's the older men who keep alive the opposition to the Gentile and all his works. The younger ones, spite all the elders tell 'em, *will* mix with the Gentile, and read Gentile books, and you bet your sweet life there's a holy influence working toward conversion in the kiss of an average Gentile—specially when the girl knows that he won't think it necessary for her salvation to load the house up with other women-folk. I guess the younger generation are giving sore trouble to the elders. What's that you say about polygamy? It's a penal offense now under a Bill passed not long ago.[2] The Mormon has to elect one wife and keep to her. If he's caught visiting any of the others—do you see that cool and restful brown stone building way over there against the hillside? That's the penitentiary. He is sent there to consider his sins, and he pays a fine, too. But most of the police in Salt Lake are Mormons, and I don't suppose they are too hard on their friends. I presoom there's a good deal of polygamy practiced on the sly. But the chief trouble is to get the Mormon to see that the Gentile isn't the doubly-damned beast that the elders represent. Only get the Gentiles well into the State, and the whole concern is bound to go to pieces in a very little time."

And the wish being father to the thought, "Why, certainly," said I, and began to take in the valley of the Desert, the home of the latterday saints, and the abode perhaps of as much misery as has ever been compressed into forty years. The good folk at home will

[2]The Edmunds Act, adopted March 22, 1882, applied severe penalties for the practice of polygamy, including fines and prison terms of up to five years. It banned polygamists from holding public office, voting, and serving on juries, and created the Utah Commission to "cleanse" Mormon institutions.

not understand, but you will, what follows. You know how in Bengal to this day the child-wife is taught to curse her possible co-wife, ere yet she has gone to her husband's house? And the Bengali woman has been accustomed to polygamy for a few hundred years. You know, too, the awful jealousy between mother wife and barren behind the purdah—the jealousy that culminates sometimes in the poisoning of the well-beloved son? Now and again, an Englishwoman employs a high-caste Mussulman nurse, and in the offices of that hire women are apt to forget the differences of color, and to speak unreservedly as twin daughters under Eve's curse. The nurse tells very strange and awful things. She has, and this the Mormons count a privilege, been born into polygamy; but she loathes and detests it from the bottom of her jealous soul. And to the lot of the Bengali co-wife—"the cursed of the cursed—the daughter of the dung-hill—the scald-head and the barren-mute" (you know the rest of that sweet commination-service)—one creed, of all the White creeds to-day, deliberately introduces the white woman taken from centuries of training, which have taught her that it is right to control the undivided heart of one man. To quench her most natural rebellion, that amazing creed and fantastic jumble of Mahometanism, the Mosaic law, and imperfectly comprehended fragments of Freemasonry, calls to its aid all the powers of a hell conceived and elaborated by coarse-minded hedgers and ditchers. A sweet view, isn't it?

All the beauty of the valley could not make me forget it. But the valley is very fair. Bench after bench of land, flat as a table against the flanks of the ringing hills, marks where the Salt Lake rested for a while as it sunk from an inland sea to a lake fifty miles long and thirty broad. Before long the benches will be covered with houses. At present these are hidden among the green trees on the dead flat of the valley. You have read a hundred time how the streets of Salt Lake City are very broad, furnished with rows of shade trees and gutters of fresh water. This is true, but I struck the town in a season of great drouth—that same drouth which is playing havoc with the herds of Montana. The trees were limp, and the rills of sparkling water that one reads about were represented by dusty, paved courses. Main

Street appears to be inhabited by the commercial Gentile, who has made of it a busy, bustling thoroughfare, and, in the eye of the sun, swigs the ungodly lager and smokes the improper cigar all day long. For which I like him. At the head of Main Street stand the lions of the place; the Temple and the Tabernacle, the Tithing House, and the houses of Brigham Young, whose portrait is on sale in most of the booksellers' shops. Incidentally it may be mentioned that the late Amir of Utah does not unremotely resemble His Highness the Amir of Afghanistan, whom these fortunate eyes have seen. And I have no desire to fall into the hands of the Amir. The first thing to be seen was, of course, the outward exponent of a creed. Armed with a copy of the Book of Mormon, for better comprehension, I went to form rash opinions. Some day the Temple will be finished. It was begun only thirty years ago, and up to date rather more than three million dollars and a half have been expended in its granite bulk. The walls are ten feet thick; the edifice itself is about a hundred feet high; and its towers will be nearly two hundred. And that is all there is of it, unless you choose to inspect more closely; always reading the Book of Mormon as you walk. Then the wondrous puerility, of what I suppose we must call the design, becomes apparent. These men, directly inspired from on High, heaped stone on stone and pillar on pillar, without achieving either dignity, relief, or interest. There is, over the main door, some pitiful scratching in stone representing the all-seeing eye, the Masonic grip, the sun, moon, and stars, and, perhaps, other skittles. The flatness and meanness of the thing almost makes you weep when you look at the magnificent granite in blocks strewn abroad, and think of the art that three million dollars might have called in to the aid of the church. It is as though a child had said: "Let us draw a great, big, fine house—finer than any house that ever was,"—and in that desire had laboriously smudged along with a ruler and pencil, piling meaningless straight lines on compass-drawn curves, with his tongue following every movement of the inept hand. Then sat I down on a wheelbarrow and read the Book of Mormon, and behold the spirit of the book was the spirit of the stone before me. The estimable Joseph and Hyrum Smith struggling to create a new

118

Bible, when they knew nothing of the history of the Old and New Testament, and the inspired architect muddling with his bricks—they were brothers. But the book was more interesting than the building. It is written, and all the world has read, how to Joseph Smith an angel came down from Heaven with a pair of celestial gig-lamps, whereby he was marvelously enabled to interpret certain plates of gold scribbled over with dots and scratches, and discovered by him in the ground. Which plates Joseph Smith did translate—only he spelt the mysterious characters "caractors"—and out of the dots and scratches produced a volume of six hundred closely printed pages, containing the books of Nephi, first and second, Jacob, Enos, Jarom, Omni, Mormon, Mosiah, the Record of Zeniff, the book of Alma Helaman, the third of Nephi, the book of Ether (the whole thing is a powerful anaesthetic, by the way), and the final book of Moroni. Three men, of whom one I believe is now living, bear solemn witness that the angel with the spectacles appeared unto them; eight other men swear solemnly that they have seen the golden plates of the revelation; and upon this testimony the book of Mormon stands. The Mormon Bible begins at the days of Zedekiah, King of Judah, and ends in a wild and weltering quagmire of tribal fights, bits of revelation, and wholesale cribs from the Bible. Very sincerely did I sympathize with the inspired brothers as I waded through their joint production. As a humble fellow-worker in the field of fiction, I knew what it was to get good names for one's characters. But Joseph and Hyrum were harder bestead than ever I have been; and bolder men to boot. They created Teancum and Coriantumy Pahoran, Kishkumen, and Gadianton, and other priceless names which the memory does not hold; but of geography they wisely steered clear, and were astutely vague as to the locality of places, because you see they were by no means certain what lay in the next country to their own. They marched and countermarched bloodthirsty armies across their pages; and added new and amazing chapters to the records of the New Testament, and reorganized the heavens and the earth as it is always lawful to do in print. But they could not achieve style, and it was foolish of them to let into their weird Mosaic pieces of the genuine Bible whenever the laboring pen dropped from its toilsome parody to a sentence or two of vile, bad English or downright "penny dreadfulism." "And Moses said unto the people of Israel: 'Great Scott! what air you doing?'" There is no sentence in the Book of Mormon word for word like the foregoing; but the general tone is not widely different.

There are the makings of a very fine creed about Mormonism. To begin with, the Church is rather more absolute than that of Rome. Drop the polygamy plank in the platform, but on the other hand deal lightly with certain forms of excess. Keep the quality of the recruits down to a low mental level and see that the best of the agricultural science available is in the hands of the Elders, and you have there a first-class engine for pioneer work. The tawdry mysticism and the borrowings from Freemasonry serve the low-caste Swede and the Dane, the Welshman and the Cornish cottar, just as well as a highly organized Heaven.

I went about the streets and peeped into people's front windows, and the decorations upon the tables were after the manner of the year 1850. Main Street was full of country folk from the outside come in to trade with the Zion Mercantile Co-operative Institute. The Church, I fancy, looks after the finances of this thing, and it consequently pays good dividends. The faces of the women were not lovely. Indeed, but for the certainty that ugly persons are just as irrational in the matter of undivided love as the beautiful, it seemed that polygamy was a blessed institution for the women, and that only the spiritual power could drive the hulking, board-faced men into it. The women wore hideous garments, and the men seemed to be tied up with string. They would market all that afternoon, and on Sunday go to the praying-place. I tried to talk to a few of them, but they spoke strange tongues and stared and behaved like cows. Yet one woman, and not an altogether ugly one, confided to me that she hated the idea of Salt Lake City being turned into a show-place for the amusement of the Gentile.

"If we 'ave our own institutions, that ain't no reason why people should come 'ere and stare at us, his it?"

The dropped "h" betrayed her.

"And when did you leave England?" I said.

"Summer of '84. I am from Dorset," she said. "The Mormon agents was very good to us, and we was very poor. Now we're better off—my father an' mother an' me."

"Then you like the State?"

She misunderstood at first. "Oh, I ain't livin' in the state of polygamy. Not me yet. I ain't married. I like where I am. I've got things o' my own—and some land."

"But I suppose you will——"

"Not me. I ain't like them Swedes an' Danes. I ain't got nothing to say for or against polygamy. It's the Elder's business, an' between you an' me I don't think it's going on much longer. You'll 'ear them in the 'ouse to-morrer talkin' as if it was spreadin' all over America. The Swedes they think it *his*. I know it hisn't."

"But you've got your land all right."

"Oh, yes, we've got our land an' we never say aught against polygamy o' course—father an' mother an' me."

It strikes me that there is a fraud somewhere. You've never heard of the rice-Christians, have you?

I should have liked to have spoken to the maiden at length, but she dived into the Zion Co-op, and a man captured me, saying that it was my bounden duty to see the sights of Salt Lake. These comprised the egg-shaped Tabernacle, the Beehive, and town houses of Brigham Young; the same great ruffian's tomb with assorted samples of his wives sleeping round him (just as the eleven faithful ones sleep round the ashes of Runjit Singh outside Fort Lahore), and one or two other curiosities. But all these things have been described by abler pens than mine. The animal-houses where Brigham used to pack his wives are grubby villas; the Tabernacle is a shingled fraud, and the Tithing House where all the revenue returns seem to be made, much resembles a stable. The Mormons have a paper currency of their own—ecclesiastical bank-notes which are exchanged for local produce. But the little boys of the place prefer the bullion of the Gentiles. It is not pleasant to be taken round a township with your guide stopping before every third house to say "That's where Elder so and so kept Amelia Bathershins, his fifth wife—no, his third. Amelia she was took on after Keziah, but Keziah was the Elder's pet, an' he didn't dare to let Amelia come across Keziah for fear of her spilin' Keziah's beauty." The Mussulmans are quite right. The minute that all the domestic details of polygamy are discussed in the mouths of the people, that institution is ready to fall. I shook off my guide when he had told me his very last doubtful tale, and went on alone. An ordered peace and a perfection of quiet luxury is the note of the city of Salt Lake. The houses stand in generous and well-groomed grass-plots, none very much worse or better than their neighbors. Creepers grow over the house fronts, and there is a very pleasant music of wind among the trees in the vast empty streets bringing a smell of hay and the flowers of summer.

On a tableland overlooking all the city stands the United States garrison of infantry and artillery. The State of Utah[3] can do nearly anything it pleases until that much-to-be-desired hour when the Gentile vote shall quietly swamp out Mormonism; but the garrison is kept there in case of accidents. The big, shark-mouthed, pig-eared, heavy-boned farmers sometimes take to their creed with wildest fanaticism, and in past years have made life excessively unpleasant for the Gentile when he was few in the land. But to-day, so far from killing openly or secretly, or burning Gentile farms, it is all the Mormon dares do to feebly try to boycott the interloper. His journals preach defiance to the United States Government, and in the Tabernacle of a Sunday the preachers follow suit. When I went down there the place was full of people who would have been much better for a washing. A man rose up and told them that they were the chosen of God, the elect of Israel that they were to obey their priest, and that there was a good time coming. I fancy that they had heard all this before so many times it produced no impression whatever; even as the sublimest mysteries of another Faith lost salt through constant iteration. They breathed heavily through their noses and stared straight in front of them—impassive as flatfish.

[3]When Kipling visited Utah during 1889, it was not yet a state. Utah Territory was admitted to the Union on January 4, 1896.

And that evening I went up to the garrison post—one of the most coveted of all the army commands—and overlooked the City of the Saints as it lay in the circle of its forbidding hills. You can speculate a good deal about the mass of human misery, the loves frustrated, the gentle hearts broken, and the strong souls twisted from the law of life to a fiercer following of the law of death, that the hills have seen. How must it have been in the old days when the footsore emigrants broke through into the circle and knew that they were cut off from hope of return or sight of friends—were handed over to the power of the friends that called themselves priests of the Most High? "But for the grace of God there goes Richard Baxter," as the eminent divine once said. It seemed good that fate did not order me to be a brick in the up-building of the Mormon church, that has so aptly established herself by the borders of a lake bitter, salt, and hopeless.

XII

"Much have I seen,
Cities and men."

Let there be no misunderstanding about the matter. I love these
People, and if any contemptuous criticism has to be done, I
will do it myself. My heart has gone out to them beyond all
other peoples; and for the life of me I cannot tell why. They
are bleeding-raw at the edges, almost more conceited than the
English, vulgar with a massive vulgarity which is as though the
Pyramids were coated with Christmas-cake sugar-works. Cocksure they are, lawless and as casual as they are cocksure; but
I love them, and I realized it when I met an Englishman who
laughed at them. He proved conclusively that they were all wrong,
from their tariff to their go-as-you-please Civil Service, and beneath the consideration of a true Briton.

"I admit everything," said I. "Their Government's provisional;
their law's the notion of the moment; their railways are made of
hairpins and matchsticks, and most of their good luck lives in
their woods and mines and rivers and not in their brains; but
for all that, they be the biggest, finest, and best people on the
surface of the globe! Just you wait a hundred years and see how
they'll behave when they've had the screw put on them and have
forgotten a few of the patriarchal teachings of the late Mister
George Washington. Wait till the Anglo-American-German-Jew
—the Man of the Future—is properly equipped. He'll have just
the least little kink in his hair now and again; he'll carry the
English lungs above the Teuton feet that can walk forever; and he
will wave long, thin bony Yankee hands with the big blue veins
on the wrist, from one end of the earth to the other. He'll be
the finest writer, poet, and dramatist, 'specially dramatist, that
the world as it recollects itself has ever seen. By virtue of his

Jew blood—just a little, little drop—he'll be a musician and a painter too. At present there is too much balcony and too little Romeo in the life-plays of his fellow-citizens. Later on, when the proportion is adjusted and he sees the possibilities of his land, he will produce things that will make the effete East stare. He will also be a complex and highly composite administrator. There is nothing known to man that he will not be, and his country will sway the world with one foot as a man tilts a seesaw plank!"

"But this is worse than the Eagle at its worst. Do you seriously believe all that?" said the Englishman.

"If I believe anything seriously, all this I most firmly believe. You wait and see. Sixty million people, chiefly of English instincts, who are trained from youth to believe that nothing is impossible, don't slink through the centuries like Russian peasantry. They are bound to leave their mark somewhere, and don't you forget it."

But isn't it sad to think that with all Eternity behind and before us we cannot, even though we would pay for it with sorrow, filch from the Immensities one hundred poor years of life, wherein to watch the two Great Experiments? A hundred years hence India and America will be worth observing. At present the one is burned out and the other is only just stoking up. When I left my opponent there was much need for faith, because I fell into the hands of a perfectly delightful man whom I had met casually in the street, sitting in a chair on the pavement, smoking a huge cigar. He was a commercial traveler, and his beat lay through Southern Mexico, and he told me tales of forgotten cities, stone gods up to their sacred eyes in forest growth, Mexican priests, rebellions, and dictatorships, that made my hair curl. It was he who dragged me forth to bathe in Salt Lake, which is some fifteen miles away from the city, and reachable by many trains which are but open tram-cars. The track, like all American tracks, was terrifying in its roughness; and the end of the journey disclosed the nakedness of the accommodation. There were piers and band houses and refreshment stalls built over the solid gray levels of the lake, but they only accentuated the utter barrenness of the place. Americans don't mix with their scenery as yet.

And "Have faith," said the commercial traveler as he walked into the water heavy as quicksilver. "Walk!" I walked, and I walked till my legs flew up and I had to walk as one struggling with a high wind, but still I rode head and shoulders above the water. It was a horrible feeling, this inability to sink. Swimming was not much use. You couldn't get a grip of the water, so I e'en sat me down and drifted like a luxurious anemone among the hundreds that were bathing in that place. You could wallow for three-quarters of an hour in that warm, sticky brine, and fear no evil consequences; but when you came out you were coated with white salt from top to toe. And if you accidentally swallowed a mouthful of the water, you died. This was true, because I swallowed half a mouthful and was half-dead in consequence.

The commercial traveler on our return journey across the level flats that fringe the lake's edge bade me note some of the customs of his people. The great open railway car held about a hundred men and maidens, "coming up with a song from the sea." They sang and they shouted and they exchanged witticisms of the most poignant, and comported themselves like their brothers and sisters over the seas—the 'Arries and 'Arriets of the older world. And there sat behind me two modest maidens in white, alone and unattended. To these the privileged youth of the car —a youth of a marvelous range of voice—proffered undying affection. They laughed, but made no reply in words. The suit was renewed, and with extravagant imagery; the nearest seats applauding. When we arrived at the city the maidens turned and went their way up a dark tree-shaded street, and the boys elsewhere. Whereat, recollecting what the London rough was like, I marveled that they did not pursue. "It's all right," said the commercial traveler. "If they had followed—well, I guess some one would ha' shot 'em." The very next day on those very peaceful cars returning from the Lake some one was shot—dead. He was what they call a "sport," which is American for a finished "leg," and he had an argument with a police officer, and the latter slew him. I saw his funeral go down the main street. There were nearly thirty carriages, filled with doubtful men, and women not in the least doubtful, and the local papers said that deceased had its merits, but it didn't much matter, because if the Sheriff hadn't dropped him he would assuredly have dropped the Sheriff. Somehow this jarred on my sensitive feelings, and I went away, though the commercial traveler would fain have entertained me in his own house, he knowing not my name. Twice through the long hot nights we talked, tilting up our chairs on the sidewalk, of the future of America.

You should hear the Saga of the States reeled off by a young and enthusiastic citizen who had just carved out for himself a home, filled it with a pretty little wife, and is preparing to embark on commerce on his own account. I was tempted to believe that pistol-shots were regrettable accidents and lawlessness only the top scum on the great sea of humanity. I am tempted to believe that still, though baked and dusty Utah is very many miles behind me.

Then chance threw me into the arms of another and very different commercial traveler, as we pulled out of Utah on our way to Omaha *via* the Rockies. He traveled in biscuits, of which more anon, and Fate had smitten him very heavily, having at one stroke knocked all the beauty and joy out of his poor life. So he journeyed with a case of samples as one dazed, and his eyes took no pleasure in anything that he saw. In his despair he had withdrawn himself to his religion,—he was a Baptist,—and spoke of its consolation with the artless freedom that an American generally exhibits when he is talking about his most sacred private affairs. There was a desert beyond Utah, hot and barren as Mian Mir in May. The sun baked the car-roof, and the dust caked the windows, and through the dust and the glare the man with the biscuits bore witness to his creed, which seems to include one of the greatest miracles in the world—the immediate unforeseen, self-conscious redemption of the soul by means very similar to those which turned Paul to the straight path.

"You must experi*ence* religion," he repeated, his mouth twitching and his eyes black-ringed with his recent loss. "You must experi*ence* religion. You can't tell when you're goin' to get, or

127

haow; but it will come—it will come, Sir, like a lightning stroke, an' you will wrestle with yourself before you receive full conviction and assurance."

"How long does that take?" I asked reverently.

"It may take hours. It may take days. I knew a man in San Jo who lay under conviction for a month an' then he got the sperrit—as you *must* git it."

"And then?"

"And then you are saved. You feel that, an' you kin endure anything," he sighed. "Yes, anything. I don't care what it is, though I allow that some things are harder than others."

"Then you have to wait for the miracle to be worked by powers outside yourself."

"And if the miracle doesn't work?"

"But it *must*. It comes to all who profess with faith."

I learned a good deal about that creed as the train fled on; and I wondered as I learned. It was a strange thing to watch that poor human soul, broken and bowed by its loss, nerving itself against each new pang of pain with the iterated assurance that it was safe against the pains of Hell.

The heat was stifling. We quitted the desert and launched into the rolling green plains of Colorado. Dozing uneasily with every removable rag removed, I was roused by a blast of intense cold and the drumming of a hundred drums. The train had stopped. Far as the eye could range the land was white under two feet of hail—each hailstone as big as the top of a sherry-glass. I saw a young colt by the side of the track standing with his poor little fluffy back to the pitiless pelting. He was pounded to death. An old horse met his doom on the run. He galloped wildly towards the train, but his hind legs dropped into a hole half water and half ice. He beat the ground with his fore-feet for a minute and then rolling over on his side submitted quietly to be killed.

When the storm ceased, we picked our way cautiously and crippledly over a track that might give way at any moment. The Western driver urges his train much as does the Subaltern the bounding pony, and 'twould seem with an equal sense of responsibility. If a foot does go wrong, why there you are, don't you know, and if it is all right, why all right it is, don't you know. But I would sooner be on the pony than the train.

This seems a good place wherein to preach on American versatility. When Mr. Howells writes a novel, when a reckless hero dams a flood by heaving a dynamite-shattered mountain into it, or when a notoriety-hunting preacher marries a couple in a balloon, you shall hear the great American press rise on its hind legs and walk round mouthing over the versatility of the American citizen. And he is versatile—horribly so. The unlimited exercise of the right of private judgment (which by the way, is a weapon not one man in ten is competent to handle), his blatant cocksureness, and the dry-air-bred restlessness that makes him crawl all over the furniture when he is talking to you, conspire to make him versatile. But what he calls versatility the impartial bystander of Anglo-Indian extraction is apt to deem mere casualness, and dangerous casualness at that. No man can grasp the inwardness of an employ by the light of pure reason—even though that reason be republican. He must serve an apprenticeship to one craft and learn that craft all the days of his life if he wishes to excel therein. Otherwise he merely "puts the thing through somehow;" and occasionally he doesn't. But wherein lies the beauty of this form of mental suppleness? Old man California, whom I shall love and respect always, told me one or two anecdotes about American versatility and its consequences that came back to my mind with direful force as the rain progressed. We didn't upset, but I don't think that was the fault of the driver or the men who made the track. Take up—you can easily find them—the accounts of ten consecutive railway catastrophes—not little accidents, but first-class fatalities, when the long cars turn over, take fire, and roast the luckless occupants alive. To seven out of the ten you shall find appended the cheerful statement: "The accident is supposed to have been due to the rails spreading." That means the metals were spiked down to the ties with such versatility that the spikes or the tracks drew under the constant vibration of the traffic, and the metals opened out. No one is hanged for these little affairs.

We began to climb hills, and then we stopped—at night in

darkness, while men threw sand under the wheels and crow-barred the track and then "guessed" that we might proceed. Not being in the least anxious to face my Maker half asleep and rubbing my eyes, I went forward to a common car, and was re-warded by two hours' conversation with the stranded, broken-down, husband-abandoned actress of a fourth-rate stranded, broken-down, manager-bereft company. She was muzzy with beer, reduced to her last dollar, fearful that there would be no one to meet her in Omaha, and wept at intervals because she had given the conductor a five-dollar bill to change, and he hadn't come back. He was an Irishman, so I knew he couldn't steal, and I addressed myself to the task of consolation. I was rewarded, after a decent interval, by the history of a life so wild, so mixed, so desperately improbable, and yet so simply probable, and above all so quick—not fast—in its kaleidoscopic changes that the *Pioneer* would reject any summary of it. And so you will never know how she, the beery woman with the tangled blond hair, was once a girl on a farm in far-off New Jersey. How he, a traveling actor, had wooed and won her,—"but Paw he was always set against Alf,"—and how he and she embarked all their little capital on the word of a faithless manager who disbanded his company a hundred miles from nowhere, and how she and Alf and a third person who had not yet made any noise in the world, had to walk the railway-track and beg from the farm-houses; how that third person arrived and went away again with a wail, and how Alf took to whisky and other things still more calculated to make a wife unhappy; and how after barn-stormings, insults, shooting-scrapes, and pitiful collapses of poor companies she had once won an encore. It was not a cheerful tale to listen to. There was a real actress in the Pullman,—such an one as travels sumptuously with a maid and dressing-case—and my draggle-tail thought of appealing to her for help, but broke down after several attempts to walk into the car jauntily as befitted a sister in the profession. Then the conductor reappeared,—the five-dollar bill honestly changed,—and she wept by reason of beer and gratitude together, and then fell asleep waveringly, alone in the car, and became almost beautiful and quite kissable; while the Man with the Sorrow stood at the door between actress and actress and preached grim sermons on the certain end of each if they did not mend their ways and find regeneration through the miracle of the Baptist creed. Yes, we were a queer company going up to the Rockies together. I was the luckiest because when a breakdown occurred, and we were delayed for twelve hours, I ate all the Baptist's sample-biscuits. They were various in composition, but nourishing. Always travel with a "drummer."

XIII

After much dallying and more climbing we came to a pass like all the Bolan Passes in the world, and the Black Cañon of the Gunnison called they it. We had been climbing for very many hours, and attained a modest elevation of some seven or eight thousand feet above the sea, when we entered a gorge, remote from the sun, where the rocks were two thousand feet sheer, and where a rock-splintered river roared and howled ten feet below a track which seemed to have been built on the simple principle of dropping miscellaneous dirt into the river and pinning a few rails atop. There was a glory and a wonder and a mystery about that mad ride which I felt keenly (you will find it properly dressed up in the guide-books), until I had to offer prayers for the safety of the train. There was no hope of seeing the track two hundred yards ahead. We seemed to be running into the bowels of the earth at the invitation of an irresponsible stream. Then the solid rock would open and disclose a curve of awful twistfulness. Then the driver put on all steam, and we would go round that curve on one wheel chiefly, the Gunnison River gnashing its teeth below. The cars overhung the edge of the water, and if a single one of the rails had chosen to spread, nothing in the wide world could have saved us from drowning. I knew we should damage something in the end—the somber horrors of the gorge, the rush of the jade-green water below, and the cheerful tales told by the conductor made me certain of the catastrophe.

We had just cleared the Black Cañon and another gorge, and were sailing out into open country nine thousand feet above the level of the sea, when we came most suddenly round a corner upon a causeway across a waste water—half dam and half quarry-pool. The locomotive gave one wild "Hoo! Hoo! Hoo!" but it was too late. He was a beautiful bull, and goodness only knows why he had chosen the track for a constitutional with his wife. She was flung to the left, but the cow-catcher caught him, and turning him round, heaved him shoulder deep into the pool. The expression of blank, blind bewilderment on his bovine, jovine face was wonderful to behold. He was not angry. I don't think he was even scared, though he must have flown ten yards through the air. All he wanted to know was: "Will somebody have the goodness to tell a respectable old gentleman what in the world, or out of it, has occurred?" And five minutes later the stream that had been snapping at our heels in the gorges split itself into a dozen silver threads on a breezy upland, and became an innocent trout beck, and we halted at a half-dead city, the name of which does not remain with me. It had originally been built on the crest of a wave of prosperity. Once ten thousand people had walked its streets; but the boom had collapsed. The great brick houses and the factories were empty. The population lived in little timber shanties on the fringes of the deserted town. There were some railway workshops and things, and the hotel (whose pavement formed the platform of the railway) contained one hundred and more rooms—empty. The place, in its half-inhabitedness, was more desolate than Amber or Chitor. But a man said: "Trout—six pounds—two miles away," and the Sorrowful Man and myself went in search of 'em. The town was ringed by a circle of hills all alive with little thunder-storms that broke across the soft green of the plain in wisps and washes of smoke and amber.

To our tiny party associated himself a lawyer from Chicago. We foregathered on the question of flies, but I didn't expect to meet Elijah Pogram in the flesh. He delivered orations on the future of England and America, and of the Great Federation that the years will bring forth when America and England will belt the globe with their linked hands. According to the notions of the British, he made an ass of himself, but for all his high-falutin he talked sense. I might knock through England on a four months' tour and not find a man capable of putting into words the passionate patriotism that possessed the little Chicago lawyer. And he was a man with points, for he offered me three days' shooting in Illinois, if I would step out of my path a little. I might travel for ten years up and down England ere I found a man who would give a complete stranger so much as a sandwich, and for twenty ere I squeezed as much enthusiasm out of a Britisher. He and I talked politics and trout-flies all one sultry day as we wandered up and down the shallows of the stream aforesaid. Little fish are sweet. I spent two hours whipping a ripple for a fish that I knew was there, and in the pasture-scented dusk caught a three-pounder on a ragged old brown hackle and landed him after ten minutes' excited argument. He was a beauty. If ever any man works the Western trout-streams, he would do well to bring out with him the dingiest flies he possesses. The natives laugh at the tiny English hooks, but they hold, and duns and drabs and sober grays seem to tickle the aesthetic tastes of the trout. For salmon (but don't say that I told you) use the spoon— gold on one side, silver on the other. It is as killing as is a similar article with fish of another caliber. The natives seem to use much too coarse tackle.

It was a search for a small boy who should know the river that revealed to me a new phase of life—slack, slovenly, and shiftless, but very interesting. There was a family in a packing-case hut on the outskirts of the town. They had seen the city when it was on the boom and made pretense of being the me-tropolis of the Rockies; and when the boom was over, they did not go. She was affable, but deeply coated with dirt; he was grim and grimy, and the little children were simply caked with filth of various descriptions. But they lived in a certain sort of squalid luxury, six or eight of them in two rooms; and they enjoyed the local society. It was their eight-year-old son whom I tried to take out with me, but he had been catching trout all his life and "guessed he didn't feel like coming," though I prof-fered him six shillings for what ought to have been a day's plea-suring. "I'll stay with Maw," he said, and from that attitude I could not move him. Maw didn't attempt to argue with him. "If he says he won't come, he won't," she said, as though he were one of the elemental forces of nature instead of a spankable brat; and "Paw," lounging by the store, refused to interfere. Maw told me that she had been a school-teacher in her not-so-distant youth, but did not tell me what I was dying to know—how she arrived at this mucky tenement at the back of beyond and why.

Though preserving the prettiness of her New England speech, she had come to regard washing as a luxury. Paw chewed tobacco and spat from time to time. Yet, when he opened his mouth for other purposes, he spoke like a well-educated man. There was a story there, but I couldn't get at it.

Next day the Man with the Sorrow and myself and a few others began the real ascent of the Rockies; up to that time our climbing didn't count. The train ran violently up a steep place and was taken to pieces. Five cars were hitched on to two locomotives, and two cars to one locomotive. This seemed to be a kind and thoughtful act, but I was idiot enough to go forward and watch the coupling-on of the two rear cars in which Caesar and his fortunes were to travel. Some one had lost or eaten the regularly ordained coupling, and a man picked up from the tailboard of the engine a single iron link about as thick as a fetterlink watch-chain, and "guessed it would do." Get hauled up a Simla cliff by the hook of a lady's parasol if you wish to appreciate my sentiments when the cars moved uphill and the link drew tight. Miles away and two thousand feet above our heads rose the shoulder of a hill epauletted with the long line of a snowtunnel. The first section of the cars crawled a quarter of a mile ahead of us, the track snaked and looped behind and there was a black drop to the left. So we went up and up and up till the thin air grew thinner and the *chunk-chunk-chunk* of the laboring locomotive was answered by the oppressed beating of the exhausted heart. Through the checked light and shade of the snow tunnels (horrible caverns of rude timbering) we ground our way, halting now and again to allow a down-train to pass. One monster of forty mineral cars slid past, scarce held by four locomotives, their brakes screaming and chortling in chorus; and in the end, after a glimpse of half America spread mapwise leagues below us, we halted at the head of the longest snow tunnel of all, on the crest of the divide, between ten and eleven thousand feet above the level of the sea. The locomotive wished to draw breath, and the passengers to gather the flowers that nodded impertinently through the chinks of the boarding. A lady passenger's nose began to bleed, and other ladies threw themselves down on the seats

135

and gasped with the gasping train, while a wind as keen as a knife-edge rioted down the grimy tunnel.

Then, despatching a pilot-engine to clear the way, we began the downward portion of the journey with every available brake on, and frequent shrieks, till after some hours we reached the level plain, and later the city of Denver, where the Man with the Sorrow went his way and left me to journey on to Omaha alone, after one hasty glance at Denver. The pulse of that town was too like the rushing mighty wind in the Rocky Mountain tunnel. It made me tired because complete strangers desired me to do something to mines which were in mountains, and to purchase building blocks upon inaccessible cliffs; and once, a woman urged that I should supply her with strong drinks. I had almost forgotten that such attacks were possible in any land, for the outward and visible signs of public morality in American towns are generally safe-guarded. For that I respect this people. Omaha, Nebraska, was but a halting-place on the road to Chicago, but it revealed to me horrors that I would not willingly have missed. The city to casual investigations seems to be populated entirely by Germans, Poles, Slavs, Hungarians, Croats, Magyars, and all the scum of Eastern European States, but it must have been laid out by Americans. No other people would cut the traffic of a main street with two streams of railway lines, each some eight or nine tracks wide, and cheerfully drive tram-cars across the metals. Every now and again they have horrible railway crossing accidents at Omaha, but nobody seems to think of building an overhead-bridge. That would interfere with the vested interests of the undertakers.

Be blessed to hear some details of one of that class.

There was a shop the like of which I had never seen before: its windows were filled with dress-coats for men, and dresses for women. But the studs of the shirts were made of stamped cloth upon the shirt front, and there were no trousers to those coats— nothing but a sweep of cheap black cloth, falling like an abbé's frock. In the doorway sat a young man reading Pollock's *Course of Time,* and by that I knew that he was an undertaker. His name was Gring, which is a beautiful name, and I talked to him on the mysteries of his Craft. He was an enthusiast and an artist. I told him how corpses were burnt in India. Said he: "We're vastly superior. We hold—that is to say, embalm—our dead. So!" Whereupon he produced the horrible weapons of his trade, and most practically showed me how you "held" a man back from that corruption which is his birthright. "And I wish I could live a few generations just to see how my people keep. But I'm sure it's all right. Nothing can touch 'em after I've embalmed 'em." Then he displayed one of those ghastly dress-suits, and when I laid a shuddering hand upon it, behold it crumpled to nothing, for the white linen was sewn on to the black cloth and—there was no back to it! That was the horror. The garment was a shell. "We dress a man in that," said Gring, laying it out tastily on the counter. "As you see here, our caskets have a plate-glass window in front" (Oh, me, but that window in the coffin was fitted with plush like a brougham-window!), "and you don't see anything below the level of the man's waistcoat. Conse-quently. . . ." He unrolled the terrible cheap black cloth that falls down over the stark feet, and I jumped back. "Of course a man can be dressed in his own clothes if he likes, but these are the regular things: and for women look at this!" He took up the body of a high-necked dinner-dress in subdued lilac, slashed and puffed and bedeviled with black, but, like the dress-suit, backless, and below the waist turning to shroud. "That's for an old maid. But for a young girl we give white with imitation pearls round the neck. That looks very pretty through the window of the cas-ket—you see there's a cushion for the head—with flowers banked all round." Can you imagine anything more awful than to take your last rest as much of a dead fraud as ever you were a living lie—to go into the darkness one-half of you shaved, trimmed and dressed for an evening party, while the other half—the half that your friends cannot see—is enwrapped in a flapping black sheet?

I know a little about burial customs in various places in the world, and I tried hard to make Mr. Gring comprehend dimly the awful heathendom that he was responsible for—the grotes-querie—the giggling horror of it all. But he couldn't see it. Even when he showed me a little boy's last suit, he couldn't see it.

He said it was quite right to embalm and trick out and hypo-critically bedizen the poor innocent dead in their superior cush-ioned and pillowed caskets with the window in front.

Bury me cased in canvas like a fishing-rod, in the deep sea; burn me on a back-water of the Hugli with damp wood and no oil; pin me under a Pullman car and let the lighted stove do its worst; sizzle me with a fallen electric wire or whelm me in the sludge of a broken river dam; but may I never go down to the Pit grinning out of a plate-glass window, in a backless dress-coat, and the front half of a black stuff dressing-gown; not though I were "held" against the ravage of the grave for ever and ever. Amen!

XIV

"I know thy cunning and thy greed,
Thy hard, high lust and willful deed,
And all thy glory loves to tell
Of specious gifts material."

I have struck a city,—a real city,—and they call it Chicago. The other places do not count. San Francisco was a pleasure-resort as well as a city, and Salt Lake was a phenomenon. This place is the first American city I have encountered. It holds rather more than a million people with bodies, and stands on the same sort of soil as Calcutta. Having seen it, I urgently desire never to see it again. It is inhabited by savages. Its water is the water of the Hugli, and its air is dirt. Also it says that it is the "boss" town of America.

I do not believe that it has anything to do with this country. They told me to go to the Palmer House, which is a gilded and mirrored rabbit-warren, and there I found a huge wall of tessellated marble, crammed with people talking about money and spitting about everywhere. Other barbarians charged in and out of this inferno with letters and telegrams in their hands, and yet others shouted at each other. A man who had drunk quite as much as was good for him told me that this was "the finest hotel in the finest city on God Almighty's earth." By the way, when an American wishes to indicate the next county or State he says, "God A'mighty's earth." This prevents discussion and flatters his vanity.

Then I went out into the streets, which are long and flat and without end. And verily it is not a good thing to live in the East for any length of time. Your ideas grow to clash with those held by every right-thinking white man. I looked down interminable vistas flanked with nine, ten, and fifteen storied houses, and crowded with men and women, and the show impressed me with a great horror. Except in London—and I have forgotten what London is like—I had never seen so many white people together, and never such a collection of miserables. There was no color in the street and no beauty—only a maze of wire-ropes overhead and dirty stone flagging underfoot. A cab-driver volunteered to show me the glory of the town for so much an hour, and with him I wandered far. He conceived that all this turmoil and squash was a thing to be reverently admired; that it was good to huddle men together in fifteen layers, one atop of the other, and to dig holes in the ground for offices. He said that Chicago was a live town, and that all the creatures hurrying by me were engaged in business. That is to say, they were trying to make some money, that they might not die through lack of food to put into their bellies. He took me to canals, black as ink, and filled with untold abominations, and bade me watch the stream of traffic across the bridges. He then took me into a saloon, and, while I drank, made me note that the floor was covered with coins sunk into cement. A Hottentot would not have been guilty of this sort of barbarism. The coins made an effect pretty enough, but the man who put them there had no thought to beauty, and therefore he was a savage. Then my cab-driver showed me business-blocks, gay with signs and studded with fantastic and absurd advertisements of goods, and looking down the long street so adorned it was as though each vendor stood at his door howling: "For the sake of money, employ or buy of *me* and me only!" Have you ever seen a crowd at our famine relief distributions? You know then how men leap into the air, stretching out their arms above the crowd in the hope of being seen; while the women dolorously slap the stomachs of their children and whimper. I had sooner watch famine-relief than the white man engaged in what he calls legitimate competition. The one I understand. The other makes me ill. And the cabman said that these things were the proof of progress; and by that I knew he had been reading his newspaper, as every intelligent American should. The papers tell their readers in language fitted to their comprehension that the snarling together of telegraph wires, the heaving up of houses, and the making of money is progress.

I spent ten hours in that huge wilderness, wandering through scores of miles of these terrible streets, and jostling some few hundred thousand of these terrible people who talked money through their noses. The cabman left me: but after a while I picked up another man who was full of figures, and into my ears he poured them as occasion required or the big blank factories suggested. Here they turned out so many hundred thousand dollars' worth of such and such an article; there so many million other things; this house was worth so many million dollars; that one so many million more or less. It was like listening to a child babbling of its hoard of shells. It was like watching a fool playing with buttons. But I was expected to do more than listen or watch. He demanded that I should admire; and the utmost that I could say was: "Are these things so? Then I am very sorry for you." That made him angry, and he said that insular envy made me unresponsive. So you see I could not make him understand.

About four and a half hours after Adam was turned out of the garden of Eden he felt hungry, and so, bidding Eve take care that her head was not broken by the descending fruit, shinned up a cocoanut palm. That hurt his legs, cut his breast, and made him breathe heavily, and Eve was tormented with fear lest her lord should miss his footing and so bring the tragedy of this world to an end ere the curtain had fairly risen. Had I met Adam then, I should have been sorry for him. To-day I find eleven hundred thousand of his sons just as far advanced as their father in the art of getting food, and immeasurably inferior to him in that they think that their palm-trees lead straight to the skies. Consequently I am sorry in rather more than a million different ways. In our East bread comes naturally even to the poorest by a little scratching or the gift of a friend not quite so poor. In less favored countries one is apt to forget. Then I went to bed. And that was on a Saturday night.

Sunday brought me the queerest experience of all—a revelation of barbarism complete. I found a place that was officially described as a church. It was a circus really, but that the worshipers did not know. There were flowers all about the building, which was fitted up with plush and stained oak and much luxury, including twisted brass candlesticks of severest Gothic design. To these things, and a congregation of savages, entered suddenly a wonderful man completely in the confidence of their God, whom he treated colloquially and exploited very much as a newspaper reporter would exploit a foreign potentate. But, unlike the newspaper reporter, he never allowed his listeners to forget that he and not He was the center of attraction. With a voice of silver and with imagery borrowed from the auction-room, he built up for his hearers a heaven on the lines of the Palmer House (but with all the gilding real gold and all the plate-glass diamond) and set in the center of it a loud-voiced, argumentative, and very shrewd creation that he called God. One sentence at this point caught my delighted ear. It was *apropos* of some question of the Judgment Day and ran: "No! I tell you God doesn't do business that way." He was giving them a deity whom they could comprehend, in a gold and jewel heaven in which they could take a natural interest. He interlarded his performance with the slang of the streets, the counter, and the Exchange, and he said that religion ought to enter into daily life. Consequently I presume he introduced it *as* daily life—his own and the life of his friends.

Then I escaped before the blessing, desiring no benediction at such hands. But the persons who listened seemed to enjoy themselves, and I understood that I had met with a popular preacher. Later on when I had perused the sermons of a gentleman called Talmadge and some others, I perceived that I had been listening to a very mild specimen. Yet that man, with his brutal gold and silver idols, his hands-in-pockets, cigar-in-mouth, and hat-on-the-back-of-the head style of dealing with the sacred vessels would count himself spiritually quite competent to send a mission to convert the Indians. All that Sunday I listened to people who said that the mere fact of spiking down strips of iron to wood and getting a steam and iron thing to run along them was progress. That the telephone was progress, and the network of wires overhead was progress. They repeated their statements again and again. One of them took me to their city hall and board of trade works and pointed it out with pride. It was very ugly, but very big, and the streets in front of it were narrow and unclean. When

I saw the faces of the men who did business in that building I felt that there had been a mistake in their billeting.

By the way, 'tis a consolation to feel that I am not writing to an English audience. Then should I have to fall into feigned ecstasies over the marvelous progress of Chicago since the days of the great fire, to allude casually to the raising of the entire city so many feet above the level of the lake which it faces, and generally to grovel before the golden calf. But you, who are desperately poor, and therefore by these standards of no account, know things, and will understand when I write that they have managed to get a million of men together on flat land, and that the bulk of these men appear to be lower than mahajans and not so companionable as a punjabi jat after harvest. But I don't think it was the blind hurry of the people, their argot, and their grand ignorance of things beyond their immediate interests that displeased me so much as a study of the daily papers of Chicago. Imprimis, there was some sort of dispute between New York and Chicago as to which town should give an exhibition of products to be hereafter holden, and through the medium of their more dignified journals the two cities were ya-hooing and hi-yi-ing at each other like opposition newsboys. They called it humor, but it sounded like something quite different. That was only the first trouble. The second lay in the tone of the productions. Leading articles which include gems such as "Back of such and such a place," or "We noticed, Tuesday, such an event," or "don't" for "does not" are things to be accepted with thankfulness. All that made me want to cry was that, in these papers, were faithfully reproduced all the warcries and "back-talk" of the Palmer House bar, the slang of the barbers' shops, the mental elevation and integrity of the Pullman-car porter, the dignity of the Dime Museum, and the accuracy of the excited fish-wife. I am sternly forbidden to believe that the paper educates the public?

Just when the sense of unreality and oppression were strongest upon me, and when I most wanted help, a man sat at my side and began to talk what he called politics. I had chanced to pay about six shillings for a traveling-cap worth eighteen pence, and he made of the fact a text for a sermon. He said that this was a rich country

143

and that the people liked to pay two hundred per cent. on the value of a thing. They could afford it. He said that the Government imposed a protective duty of from ten to seventy per cent. on foreign made articles, and that the American manufacturer consequently could sell his goods for a healthy sum. Thus an imported hat would, with duty, cost two guineas. The American manufacturer would make a hat for seventeen shillings and sell it for one pound fifteen. In these things, he said, lay the greatness of America and the effeteness of England. Competition between factory and factory kept the prices down to decent limits, but I was never to forget that this people were a rich people, not like the pauper Continentals, and that they enjoyed paying duties. To my weak intellect this seemed rather like juggling with counters. Everything that I have yet purchased costs about twice as much as it would in England, and when native-made is of inferior quality. Moreover, since these lines were first thought of I have visited a gentleman who owned a factory which used to produce things. He owned the factory still. Not a man was in it, but he was drawing a handsome income from a syndicate of firms for keeping it closed in order that it might not produce things. This man said that if protection were abandoned, a tide of pauper labor would flood the country, and as I looked at his factory I thought how entirely better it was to have no labor of any kind whatever, rather than face so horrible a future. Meantime, do you remember that this peculiar country enjoys paying money for value not received? I am an alien, and for the life of me cannot see why six shillings should be paid for eighteen-penny caps, or eight shillings for half-crown cigar-cases. When the country fills up to a decently populated level a few million people who are not aliens will be smitten with the same sort of blindness.

But my friend's assertion somehow thoroughly suited the grotesque ferocity of Chicago. See now and judge! In the last village of Isser Jang on the road to Montgomery there be four *changar* women who winnow corn—some seventy bushels a year. Beyond their hut lives Puran Dass, the money-lender, who on good security lends as much as five thousand rupees in a year. Jowala Singh, the *lohar,* mends the village plow—some thirty, broken in the share, in three hundred and sixty-five days; and Hukm Chund, who is letter-writer and head of the little club under the travelers' tree, generally keeps the village posted in such gossip as the barber and the midwife have not yet made public property. Chicago husks and winnows her wheat by the million bushels, a hundred banks lend hundreds of millions of dollars in the year, and scores of factories turn out plow gear and machinery by steam. Scores of daily papers do work which Hukm Chund and the barber and the midwife perform, with due regard for public opinion, in the village of Isser Jang. So far as manufactures go, the difference between Chicago on the lake and Isser Jang on the Montgomery road is one of degree only, and not of kind. As far as the understanding of the uses of life goes Isser Jang, for all its seasonal cholera, has the advantage over Chicago. Jowala Singh knows and takes care to avoid the three or four ghoul-haunted fields on the outskirts of the village; but he is not urged by millions of devils to run about all day in the sun and swear that his plowshares are the best in the Punjab; nor does Puran Dass fly forth in a cart more than once or twice a year, and he knows, on a pinch, how to use the railway and the telegraph as well as any son of Israel in Chicago. But this is absurd. The East is not the West, and these men must continue to deal with the machinery of life, and to call it progress. Their very preachers dare not rebuke them. They gloss over the hunting for money and the twice-sharpened bitterness of Adam's curse by saying that such things dower a man with a larger range of thoughts and higher aspirations. They do not say: "Free yourself from your own slavery," but rather, "If you can possibly manage it, do not set quite so much store on the things of this world." And they do not know what the things of this world are.

I went off to see cattle killed by way of clearing my head, which, as you will perceive, was getting muddled. They say every Englishman goes to the Chicago stock-yards. You shall find them about six miles from the city; and once having seen them will never forget the sight. As far as the eye can reach stretches a township of cattle-pens, cunningly divided into blocks so that the animals of any pen can be speedily driven out close to an inclined timber path which leads to an elevated covered way straddling high above the pens. These viaducts are two-storied. On the upper story tramp the doomed cattle, stolidly for the most part. On the lower, with a scuffling of sharp hoofs and multitudinous yells, run the pigs. The same end is appointed for each. Thus you will see the gangs of cattle waiting their turn—as they wait sometimes for days; and they need not be distressed by the sight of their fellows running about in the fear of death. All they know is that a man on horseback causes their next-door neighbors to move by means of a whip. Certain bars and fences are unshipped, and, behold, that crowd have gone up the mouth of a sloping tunnel and return no more. It is different with the pigs. They shriek back the news of the exodus to their friends, and a hundred pens skirl responsive. It was to the pigs I first addressed myself. Selecting a viaduct which was full of them, as I could hear though I could not see, I marked a somber building whereto it ran, and went there, not unalarmed by stray cattle who had managed to escape from their proper quarters. A pleasant smell of brine warned me of what was coming. I entered the factory and found it full of pork in barrels, and on another story more pork unbarreled, and in a huge room, the halves of swine for whose use great lumps of ice were being pitched in at the window. That room was the mortuary chamber where the pigs lie for a little while in state ere they begin their progress through such passages as kings may sometimes travel. Turning a corner and not noting an overhead arrangement of greased rail, wheel, and pulley, I ran into the arms of four eviscerated carcasses, all pure white and of a human aspect, being pushed by a man clad in vehement red. When I leaped aside, the floor was slippery under me. There was a flavour of farmyard in my nostrils and the shouting of a multitude in my ears. But there was no joy in that shouting. Twelve men stood in two lines—six aside. Between them and overhead ran the railway of death that had nearly shunted me through the window. Each man carried a knife, the sleeves of his shirt were cut off at the elbows, and from bosom to heel he was blood-red. The atmosphere was stifling as a night in the Rains, by reason of the steam and the crowd. I climbed to the beginning of things and, perched upon a narrow beam, overlooked very nearly all the pigs ever bred in Wisconsin. They had just been shot out of the mouth of the viaduct and huddled together in a large pen. Thence they were flicked persuasively, a few at the time, into a smaller chamber, and there a man fixed tackle on their hinder legs so that they rose in the air suspended from the railway of death. Oh! it was then they shrieked and called on their mothers and made promises of amendment, till the tackle-man punted them in their backs, and they slid head down into a brick-floored passage, very like a big kitchen sink that was blood-red. There awaited them a red man with a knife which he passed jauntily through their throats, and the full-voiced shriek became a sputter, and then a fall as of heavy tropical rain. The red man who was backed against the passage wall stood clear of the wildly kicking hoofs and passed his hand over his eyes, not from any feeling of compassion, but because the spurted blood was in his eyes and he had barely time to stick the next arrival. Then that first stuck swine dropped, still kicking, into a great vat of boiling water, and spoke no more words, but wallowed in obedience to some unseen machinery, and presently came forth at the lower end of the vat and was heaved on the blades of a blunt paddle-wheel-thing which said, "Hough! Hough! Hough!" and skelped all the hair off him except what little a couple of men with knives could remove. Then he was again hitched by the heels to that said railway and passed down the line of the twelve men— each with a knife—leaving with each man a certain amount of his individuality which was taken away in a wheelbarrow, and when he reached the last man he was very beautiful to behold, but immensely unstuffed and limp. Preponderance of individuality was ever a bar to foreign travel. That pig could have been in no case to visit you in India had he not parted with some of his most cherished notions.

The dissecting part impressed me not so much as the slaying. They were so excessively alive, these pigs. And then they were so excessively dead, and the man in the dripping, clammy, hot passage did not seem to care, and ere the blood of such an one had ceased to foam on the floor, such another, and four friends with him, had shrieked and died. But a pig is only the Unclean animal—forbidden by the Prophet.

I was destined to make rather a queer discovery when I went over to the cattle-slaughter. All the buildings here were on a much larger scale, and there was no sound of trouble, but I could smell the salt reek of blood before I set foot in the place. The cattle did not come directly through the viaduct as the pigs had done. They debouched into a yard by the hundred, and they were big red brutes carrying much flesh. In the center of that yard stood a red Texan steer with a headstall on his wicked head. No man controlled him. He was, so to speak, picking his teeth and whistling in an open byre of his own when the cattle arrived. As soon as the first one had fearfully quitted the viaduct, this red devil put his hands in his pockets and slouched across the yard, no man guiding him. Then he lowed something to the effect that he was the regularly appointed guide of the establishment and would show them round. They were country folk, but they knew how to behave; and so followed Judas some hundred strong, patiently, and with a look of bland wonder in their faces. I saw his broad back jogging in advance of them, up a lime-washed incline where I was forbidden to follow. Then a door shut, and in a minute back came Judas with the air of a virtuous plow-bullock and took up his place in his byre. Somebody laughed across the yard, but I heard no sound of cattle from the big brick building into which the mob had disappeared. Only Judas chewed the cud with a malignant satisfaction, and so I knew there was trouble, and ran round to the front of the factory and so entered and stood aghast.

Who takes count of the prejudices which we absorb through the skin by way of our surroundings? It was not the spectacle that impressed me. The first thought that almost spoke itself aloud was: "They are killing kine;" and it was a shock. The pigs were nobody's concern, but cattle—the brothers of the Cow, the Sacred Cow—were quite otherwise. The next time an M. P. tells me that India either Sultanizes or Brahminizes a man, I shall believe about half what he says. It is unpleasant to watch the slaughter of cattle when one has laughed at the notion for a few years. I could not see actually what was done in the first instance, because the row of stalls in which they lay was separated from me by fifty impassable feet by butchers and slung carcasses. All I know is that men swung open the doors of a stall as occasion required, and there lay two steers already stunned, and breathing heavily. These two they pole-axed, and half raising them by tackle they cut their throats. Two men skinned each carcass, somebody cut off the head, and in half a minute more the overhead rail carried two sides of beef to their appointed place. There was clamor enough in the operating room, but from the waiting cattle, invisible on the other side of the line of pens, never a sound. They went to their death, trusting Judas, without a word. They were slain at the rate of five a minute, and if the pig men were spattered with blood, the cow butchers were bathed in it. The blood ran in muttering gutters. There was no place for hand or foot that was not coated with thicknesses of dried blood, and the stench of it in the nostrils bred fear.

And then the same merciful Providence that has showered good things on my path throughout sent me an embodiment of the city of Chicago, so that I might remember it forever. Women come sometimes to see the slaughter, as they would come to see the slaughter of men. And there entered that vermilion hall a young woman of large mold, with brilliantly scarlet lips, and heavy eyebrows, and dark hair that came in a "widow's peak" on the forehead. She was well and healthy and alive, and she was dressed in flaming red and black, and her feet (know you that the feet of American women are like unto the feet of fairies?) her feet, I say, were cased in red leather shoes. She stood in a patch of sunlight, the red blood under her shoes, the vivid carcasses tacked round her, a bullock bleeding its life away not six feet away from her, and the death factory roaring all round her. She looked curiously, with hard, bold eyes, and was not ashamed.

Then said I: "This is a special Sending. I have seen the City of Chicago." And I went away to get peace and rest.

XV

It is a mean thing and an unhandsome to "do" a continent in five-hundred-mile jumps. But after those swine and bullocks at Chicago I felt the complete change of air would be good. The United States at present hinge in or about Chicago, as a double-leaved screen hinges. To be sure, the tiny New England States call a trip to Pennsylvania "going west," but the larger-minded citizen seems to reckon his longitude from Chicago. Twenty years hence the center of population—that shaded square on the census map—will have shifted, men say, far west of Chicago. Twenty years later it will be on the Pacific slope. Twenty years after that America will begin to crowd up, and there will be some trouble. People will demand manufactured goods for their reduced-establishment households at the cheapest possible rates, and the cry that the land is rich enough to afford protection will cease with a great abruptness. At present it is the farmer who pays most dearly for the luxury of high prices. In the old days, when the land was fresh and there was plenty of it and it cropped like the garden of Eden, he did not mind paying. Now there is not so much free land, and the old acres are needing stimulants, which cost money, and the farmer, who pays for everything, is beginning to ask questions. Also the great American nation, which individually never shuts a door behind its noble self, very seldom attempts to put back anything that it has taken from Nature's shelves. It grabs all it can and moves on. But the moving-on is nearly finished and the grabbing must stop, and then the Federal Government will have to establish a Woods and Forests Department the like of which was never seen in the world before. And all the people who have been accustomed to hack, mangle, and burn timber as they please will object, with shots and protestations, to this infringement of their rights. The nigger will breed bounteously, and *he* will have to be reckoned with; and the manufacturer will have to be contented with smaller profits, and *he* will have to be reckoned with; and the railways will no longer rule the countries through which they run, and they will have to be reckoned with. And nobody will approve of it in the least.

Yes; it will be a spectacle for all the world to watch, this big, slashing colt of a nation, that has got off with a flying start on a freshly littered course, being pulled back to the ruck by that very mutton-fisted jockey Necessity. There will be excitement in America when a few score millions of "sovereigns" discover that what they considered the outcome of their own Government is but the rapidly diminishing bounty of Nature; and that if they want to get on comfortably they must tackle every single problem from labor to finance humbly, without gasconade, and afresh. But at present they look "that all the tomorrows shall be as to-day," and if you argue with them they say that the Democratic Idea will keep things going. They believe in that Idea, and the less well-informed fortify themselves in their belief by curious assertions as to the despotism that exists in England. This is pure provincialism, of course; but it is very funny to listen to, especially when you compare the theory with the practice (pistol, chiefly) as proven in the newspapers. I have striven to find out where the central authority of the land lies. It isn't at Washington, because the Federal Government can't do anything to the States save run the mail and collect a Federal tax or two. It isn't in the States, because the townships can do as they like; and it isn't in the townships, because these are bossed by alien voters or rings of patriotic homebred citizens. And it certainly is not in the citizens, because they are governed and coerced by despotic power of public opinion as represented by their papers, preachers, or local society. I found one man who told me that if anything went wrong in this huge congress of kings,—if there was a split or an upheaval or a smash,—the people in detail would be subject to the Idea of the sovereign people in mass. This is a survival from the Civil War, when, you remember, the people in a majority did with guns and swords slay and wound the people in detail. All the same, the notion seems very much like the worship by the savage of the unloaded rifle as it leans against the wall.

But the men and women set Us an example in patriotism. They believe in their land and its future, and its honor, and its glory, and they are not ashamed to say so. From the largest to the least runs this same proud, passionate conviction to which I take off my hat and for which I love them. An average English householder seems to regard his country as an abstraction to supply him with policemen and fire-brigades. The cockney cad cannot understand what the word means. The bloomin' toffs he knows, and the law, and the soldiers that supply him with a spectacle in the Parks; but he would laugh in your face at the notion of any duty being owed by himself to his land. Pick an American of the second generation anywhere you please—from the cab-rank, the porter's room, or the plow-tail—'specially the plow-tail,—and that man will make you understand in five minutes that he understands what manner of thing his Republic is. He might laugh at a law that didn't suit his convenience, draw your eye-teeth in a bargain, and applaud 'cuteness on the outer verge of swindling; but you should hear him stand up and sing:—

> "My country 'tis of thee,
> Sweet land of liberty,
> Of thee I sing!"

I have heard a few thousand of them engaged in that employment. I respect him. There is too much Romeo and too little balcony about our National Anthem. With the American article it is all balcony. There must be born a poet who shall give the English *the* song of their own, own country—which is to say, of about half the world. Remains then only to compose the greatest song of all—The Saga of the Anglo-Saxon all round the earth—a paean that shall combine the terrible slow swing of the *Battle Hymn of the Republic* (which, if you know not, get chanted to you) with *Britannia needs no Bulwarks,* the skirl of the *British Grenadiers* with that perfect quick-step, *Marching through Georgia,* and at the end the wail of the *Dead March.* For We, even

We who share the earth between us as no gods have ever shared it, we also are mortal in the matter of our single selves. Will any one take the contract?

It is with these rambling notions that I arrived at the infinite peace of the tiny township of Musquash on the Monongahela River. The clang and tumult of Chicago belonged to another world. Imagine a rolling, wooded, English landscape, under softest of blue skies, dotted at three-mile intervals with fat little, quiet little villages; or aggressive little manufacturing towns that the trees and the folds of the hills mercifully prevented from betraying their presence. The golden-rod blazed in the pastures against the green of the mulleins, and the cows picked their way home through the twisted paths between the blackberry bushes. All summer was on the orchards, and the apples—such apples as we dream of when we eat the woolly imitations of Kashmir— were ripe and toothsome. It was good to lie in a hammock with half-shut eyes, and in the utter stillness, to hear the apples dropping from the trees, and the tinkle of the cowbells as the cows walked statelily down the main road of the village. Everybody in that restful place seemed to have just as much as he wanted; a house with all comfortable appliances, a big or little veranda wherein to spend the day, a neatly shaved garden with a wild wealth of flowers, some cows, and an orchard. Everybody knew everybody else intimately, and what they did not know, the local daily paper—a daily for a village of twelve hundred people!— supplied. There was a courthouse where justice was done, and a jail where some most enviable prisoners lived, and there were four or five churches of four or five denominations. Also it was impossible to buy openly any liquor in that little paradise. But— and this is a very serious *but*—you could by procuring a medical certificate get strong drinks from the chemist. That is the drawback of prohibition. It makes a man who wants a drink a shirker and a contriver, which things are not good for the soul of a man, and presently, 'specially if he be young, causes him to believe that he may just as well be hanged for a sheep as for a lamb; and the end of that young man is not pretty. Nothing except a rattling fall will persuade an average colt that a fence is not meant to be jumped over; whereas if he be turned out into the open he learns to carry himself with discretion. One heard a good deal of this same dread of drink in Musquash, and even the maidens seemed to know too much about its effects upon certain unregenerate youths, who, if they had been once made thoroughly, effectually, and persistently drunk—with a tepid brandy and soda thrust before their goose-fleshed noses on the terrible Next Morning—would perhaps have seen the futility of their ways. It was a sin by village canons to imbibe lager, though—*experto crede*—you can get dropsy on that stuff long before you can get drunk. "But what man knows his mind?" Besides, it was all their own affair.

The little community seemed to be as self-contained as an Indian village. Had the rest of the land sunk under the sea, Musquash would have gone on sending its sons to school in order to make them "good citizens," which is the constant prayer of the true American father, settling its own road-making, local cesses, town-lot arbitrations, and internal government by ballot and vote and due respect to the voices of the headmen (which is the salvation of the ballot), until such time as all should take their places in the cemetery appointed for their faith. Here were Americans and no aliens—men ruling themselves by themselves and for themselves and their wives and their children—in peace, order, and decency.

But what went straightest to this heart, though they did not know it, was that they were Methody folk for the most part—aye, Methody as ever trod a Yorkshire Moor, or drove on a Sunday to some chapel of the Faith in the Dales. The old Methody talk was there, with the discipline whereby the souls of the Just are, sometimes to their intense vexation, made perfect on this earth in order that they may "take out their letters and live and die in good standing." If you don't know the talk, you won't know what that means. The discipline, or dis*cip*line, is no thing to be trifled with, and its working among a congregation depends entirely upon the tact, humanity, and sympathy of the leader who works it. He, knowing what youth's desires are, can turn the soul in the direction of good, gently, instead of wrenching it savagely towards the right path only to see it break away quivering and scared. The arm of Dis*cip*line is long. A maiden told me, as a new and strange fact and one that would interest a foreigner, of a friend of hers who had once been admonished by some elders somewhere—not in Musquash—for the heinous crime of dancing. She, the friend, did not in the least like it. She would not. Can't you imagine the delightful results of a formal wigging administered by a youngish and austere elder who was not accustomed to make allowances for the natural dancing instincts of the young of the human animal? The hot irons that are held forth to scare may also sear, as those who have ever lain under an unfortunate exposition of the old Faith can attest.

But it was all immensely interesting—the absolutely fresh, wholesome, sweet life that paid due reverence to the things of the next world, but took good care to get enough tennis in the cool of the evening; that concerned itself as honestly and thoroughly with the daily round, the trivial task (and that same task is anything but trivial when you are "helped" by an American "help") as with the salvation of the soul. I had the honor of meeting in the flesh, even as Miss Louisa Alcott drew them, Meg and Joe and Beth and Amy, whom you ought to know. There was no affectation of concealment in their lives who had nothing to conceal. There were many "little women" in that place, because, even as is the case in England, the boys had gone out to seek their fortunes. Some were working in the thundering, clanging cities, others had removed in the infinite West, and others had disappeared in the languid, lazy South; and the maidens waited their return, which is the custom of maidens all over the world. Then the boys would come back in the soft sunlight, attired in careful raiment, their tongues cleansed of evil words and discourtesy. They had just come to call—bless their carefully groomed heads, so they had,—and the maidens in white dresses glimmered like ghosts on the stoop and received them according to their merits. Mama had nothing to do with this, nor papa either, for he was down-town trying to drive reason into the head of a land surveyor; and all along the shaded, lazy, intimate street you heard the garden-gates click and clash, as the mood of the man

varied, and bursts of pleasant laughter where three or four—
be sure the white muslins were among them,—discussed a picnic
past or a buggy-drive to come. Then the couples went their ways
and talked together till the young men had to go at last on
account of the trains, and all trooped joyously down to the
station and thought no harm of it. And, indeed, why should
they? From her fifteenth year the American maiden moves among
"the boys" as a sister among brothers. They are her servants to
take her out riding,—which is driving,—to give her flowers and
candy. The last two items are expensive, and this is good for
the young man, as teaching him to value friendship that costs
a little in cash and may necessitate economy on the cigar side.
As to the maiden, she is taught to respect herself, that her fate
is in her own hands, and that she is the more stringently bound
by the very measure of the liberty so freely accorded to her.
Wherefore, in her own language, "she has a lovely time" with
about two or three hundred boys who have sisters of their own,
and a very accurate perception that if they were unworthy of
their trust a syndicate of other boys would probably pass them
into a world where there is neither marrying nor giving in marriage. And so time goes till the maiden knows the other side of
the house,—knows that a man is not a demi-god nor a myste-
riously veiled monster, but an average, egotistical, vain, glut-
tonous, but on the whole, companionable sort of person, to be
soothed, fed and managed—knowledge that does not come to her
sister in England till after a few years of matrimony. And then
she makes her choice. The Golden Light touches eyes that are
full of comprehension; but the light is golden none the less, for
she makes just the same sweet, irrational choices that an English
girl does. With this advantage: she knows a little more, has experience in entertaining, insight into the businesses, employ, and
hobbies of men, gathered from countless talks with the boys, and
talks with the other girls who find time at those mysterious
conclaves to discuss what Tom, Ted, Stuke, or Jack have been
doing. Thus it happens that she is a companion, in the fullest
sense of the word, of the man she weds, zealous for the interest
of the firm, to be consulted in time of stress and to be called

upon for help and sympathy in time of danger. Pleasant it is that one heart should beat for you; but it is better when the head above the heart has been thinking hard on your behalf, and when the lips, that are also very pleasant to kiss, give wise counsel.

When the American maiden—I speak now for the rank and file of that noble army—is once married, why, it is finished. She has had her lovely time. It may have been five, seven, or ten years according to circumstances. She abdicates promptly with startling speed, and her place knows her no more except as with her husband. The Queen is dead, or looking after the house. This same household work seems to be the thing that ages the American woman. She is infamously "helped" by the Irish trollop and the negress alike. It is not fair upon her, because she has to do three parts of the housework herself, and in dry, nerve-straining air the "chores" are a burden. Be thankful, oh my people, for Mauz Baksh, Kadir Baksh, and the *ayah* while they are with you. They are twice as handy as the unkempt slatterns of the furnished apartments to which you will return, Commissioners though you be; and five times as clever as the Amelia Araminta Rebellia Secessia Jackson (colored) under whose ineptitude and insolence the young American housewife groans. But all this is far enough from peaceful, placid Musquash, and its boundless cordiality, its simple, genuine hospitality, and its—what's the French word that just covers all? —*gra—gracieuseness,* isn't it? Oh, be good to an American whenever you meet him. Put him up for the club, and he will hold you listening till three in the morning; give him the best tent, and the grain-fed mutton. I have incurred a debt of salt that I can never repay, but do you return it piecemeal to any of that Nation, and the account will be on my head till our paths in the world cross again. He drinks iced water just as we do; but he doesn't quite like our cigars.

And how shall I finish the tale? Would it interest you to learn of the picnics in the hot, still woods that overhang the Mononga-hela, when those idiotic American buggies that can't turn round got stuck among the brambles and all but capsized; of boating in the blazing sun on the river that but a little time before had cast at the feet of the horrified village the corpses of the Johns-town tragedy? I saw one, only one, remnant of that terrible wreck. He had been a minister. House, church, congregation, wife, and children had been swept away from him in one night of terror. He had no employment; he could have employed himself at noth-ing. But God had been very good to him. He sat in the sun and smiled a little weakly. It was in his poor blurred mind that some-thing had happened—he was not sure what it was, but undoubtedly something had occurred. One could only pray that the light would never return.

But there be many pictures on my mind. Of a huge manufac-turing city of three hundred thousand souls lighted and warmed by natural gas, so that the great valley full of flaming furnaces sent up no smoke wreaths to the clear sky. Of Musquash itself lighted by the same mysterious agency, flares of gas eight feet long, roaring day and night at the corners of the grass-grown streets because it wasn't worth while to turn them out; of fleets of coal-flats being hauled down the river on an interminable journey to St. Louis; of factories nestling in woods where all the ax-handles and shovels in the world seemed to be manu-factured daily; and last, of that quaint forgotten German com-munity, the Brotherhood of Perpetual Separation who founded themselves when the State was yet young and land cheap, and are now dying out because they will neither marry nor give in marriage and their recruits are very few. The advance in the value of land has almost smothered these poor old people in a golden affluence that they never desired. They live in a little village where the houses are built old Dutch fashion, with their front doors away from the road, and cobbled paths all about. The cloistered peace of Musquash is a metropolitan riot beside the hush of that village. And there is, too, a love-tale tucked away among the flowers. It has taken seventy years in the tell-ing, for the brother and sister loved each other well, but they loved their duty to the brotherhood more. So they have lived and still do live, seeing each other daily, and separated for all time. Any trouble that might have been is altogether wiped out of their faces, which are as calm as those of very little children.

To the uninitiated those constant ones resemble extremely old people in garments of absurd cut. But they love each other, and that seems to bring one back quite naturally to the girls and the boys in Musquash. The boys were nice boys—graduates of Yale of course; you mustn't mention Harvard here—but none the less skilled in business, in stocks and shares, the boring for oil, and the sale of everything that can be sold by one sinner to another. Skilled, too, in baseball, big-shouldered, with straight eyes and square chins—but not above occasional diversion and mild orgies. They will make good citizens and possess the earth, and eventually wed one of the nice white muslin dresses. There are worse things in this world than being "one of the boys" in Musquash.

AN INTERVIEW
WITH MARK TWAIN

You are a contemptible lot, over yonder. Some of you are Commissioners, and some Lieutenant-Governors, and some have the
V. C., and a few are privileged to walk about the Mall arm in
arm with the Viceroy; but *I* have seen Mark Twain this golden
morning, have shaken his hand, and smoked a cigar—no, two
cigars—with him, and talked with him for more than two hours!
Understand clearly that I do not despise you; indeed, I don't.
I am only very sorry for you, from the Viceroy downward. To
soothe your envy and to prove that I still regard you as my equals,
I will tell you all about it.

They said in Buffalo that he was in Hartford, Conn.; and again
they said "perchance he is gone upon a journey to Portland"; and
a big, fat drummer vowed that he knew the great man intimately,
and that Mark was spending the summer in Europe—which information so upset me that I embarked upon the wrong train, and
was incontinently turned out by the conductor three-quarters of
a mile from the station, amid the wilderness of railway tracks.
Have you ever, encumbered with greatcoat and valise, tried to
dodge diversely-minded locomotives when the sun was shining in
your eyes? But I forget that you have not seen Mark Twain, you
people of no account!

Saved from the jaws of the cow-catcher, me wandering devious
a stranger met.

"Elmira is the place. Elmira in the State of New York—this
State, not two hundred miles away;" and he added, perfectly
unnecessarily, "Slide, Kelly, slide."

I slid on the West Shore line, I slid till midnight, and they
dumped me down at the door of a frowzy hotel in Elmira. Yes, they

knew all about "that man Clemens," but reckoned he was not in town; had gone East somewhere. I had better possess my soul in patience till the morrow, and then dig up the "man Clemens'" brother-in-law, who was interested in coal.

The idea of chasing half a dozen relatives in addition to Mark Twain up and down a city of thirty thousand inhabitants kept me awake. Morning revealed Elmira, whose streets were desolated by railway tracks, and whose suburbs were given up to the manufacture of door-sashes and window-frames. It was surrounded by pleasant, fat, little hills, rimmed with timber and topped with cultivation. The Chemung River flowed generally up and down the town, and had just finished flooding a few of the main streets.

The hotel-man and the telephone-man assured me that the much-desired brother-in-law was out of town, and no one seemed to know where the "man Clemens" abode. Later on I discovered that he had not summered in that place for more than nineteen seasons, and so was comparatively a new arrival.

A friendly policeman volunteered the news that he had seen Twain or "some one very like him" driving a buggy the day before. This gave me a delightful sense of nearness. Fancy living in a town where you could see the author of "Tom Sawyer," or "some one very like him," jolting over the pavements in a buggy!

"He lives out yonder at East Hill," said the policeman; "three miles from here."

Then the chase began—in a hired hack, up an awful hill, where sunflowers blossomed by the roadside, and crops waved, and "Harper's Magazine" cows stood in eligible and commanding attitudes knee-deep in clover, all ready to be transferred to photogravure. The great man must have been persecuted by outsiders aforetime, and fled up the hill for refuge.

Presently the driver stopped at a miserable, little, white wood shanty, and demanded "Mister Clemens."

"I know he's a big-bug and all that," he explained, "but you can never tell what sort of notions those sort of men take into their heads to live in, anyways."

There rose up a young lady who was sketching thistle-tops and goldenrod, amid a plentiful supply of both, and set the pilgrimage on the right path.

"It's a pretty Gothic house on the left-hand side a little way farther on."

"Gothic h——," said the driver. "Very few of the city hacks take this drive, specially if they know they are coming out here," and he glared at me savagely.

It was a very pretty house, anything but Gothic, clothed with ivy, standing in a very big compound, and fronted by a verandah full of chairs and hammocks. The roof of the verandah was a trelliswork of creepers, and the sun peeping through moved on the shining boards below.

Decidedly this remote place was an ideal one for work, if a man could work among these soft airs and the murmur of the long-eared crops.

Appeared suddenly a lady used to dealing with rampageous outsiders. "Mr. Clemens has just walked down-town. He is at his brother-in-law's house."

Then he was within shouting distance, after all, and the chase had not been in vain. With speed I fled, and the driver, skidding the wheel and swearing audibly, arrived at the bottom of that hill without accidents. It was in the pause that followed between ringing the brother-in-law's bell and getting an answer that it occurred to me for the first time Mark Twain might possibly have other engagements than the entertainment of escaped lunatics from India, be they never so full of admiration. And in another man's house—anyhow, what had I come to do or say? Suppose the drawing-room should be full of people—suppose a baby were sick, how was I to explain that I only wanted to shake hands with him?

Then things happened somewhat in this order. A big, darkened drawing-room; a huge chair; a man with eyes, a mane of grizzled hair, brown mustache covering a mouth as delicate as a woman's, a strong, square hand shaking mine, and the slowest, calmest, levellest voice in all the world saying:—

"Well, you think you owe me something, and you've come to tell me so. That's what I call squaring a debt handsomely."

"Piff!" from a cob-pipe (I always said that a Missouri meerschaum was the best smoking in the world), and, behold! Mark

Twain had curled himself up in the big arm-chair, and I was smoking reverently, as befits one in the presence of his superior.

The thing that struck me first was that he was an elderly man; yet, after a minute's thought, I perceived that it was otherwise, and in five minutes, the eyes looking at me, I saw that the grey hair was an accident of the most trivial. He was quite young. I was shaking his hand. I was smoking his cigar, and I was hearing him talk — this man I had learned to love and admire fourteen thousand miles away.

Reading his books, I had striven to get an idea of his personality, and all my preconceived notions were wrong and beneath the reality. Blessed is the man who finds no disillusion when he is brought face to face with a revered writer. That was a moment to be remembered; the landing of a twelve-pound salmon was nothing to it. I had hooked Mark Twain, and he was treating me as though under certain circumstances I might be an equal.

About this time I became aware that he was discussing the copyright question. Here, so far as I remember, is what he said. Attend to the words of the oracle through this unworthy medium transmitted. You will never be able to imagine the long, slow surge of the drawl, and the deadly gravity of the countenance, the quaint pucker of the body, one foot thrown over the arm of the chair, the yellow pipe clinched in one corner of the mouth, and the right hand casually caressing the square chin: —

"Copyright? Some men have morals, and some men have — other things. I presume a publisher is a man. He is not born. He is created — by circumstances. Some publishers have morals. Mine have. They pay me for the English productions of my books. When you hear men talking of Bret Harte's works and other works and my books being pirated, ask them to be sure of their facts. I think they'll find the books are paid for. It was ever thus.

"I remember an unprincipled and formidable publisher. Perhaps he's dead now. He used to take my short stories — I can't call it steal or pirate them. It was beyond these things altogether. He took my stories one at a time and made a book of it. If I wrote an essay on dentistry or theology or any little thing of that kind — just an essay that long (he indicated half an inch on his finger), any sort of essay—that publisher would amend and improve my essay.

"He would get another man to write more to it or cut it about exactly as his needs required. Then he would publish a book called 'Dentistry by Mark Twain,' that little essay and some other things not mine added. Theology would make another book, and so on. I do not consider that fair. It's an insult. But he's dead now, I think. I didn't kill him.

"There is a great deal of nonsense talked about international copyright. The proper way to treat a copyright is to make it exactly like real-estate in every way.

"It will settle itself under these conditions. If Congress were to bring in a law that a man's life was not to extend over a hundred and sixty years, somebody would laugh. That law wouldn't concern anybody. The man would be out of the jurisdiction of the court. A term of years in copyright comes to exactly the same thing. No law can make a book live or cause it to die before the appointed time.

"Tottletown, Cal., was a new town, with a population of three thousand—banks, fire-brigade, brick buildings, and all the modern improvements. It lived, it flourished, and it disappeared. To-day no man can put his foot on any remnant of Tottletown, Cal. It's dead. London continues to exist. Bill Smith, author of a book read for the next year or so, is real-estate in Tottletown. William Shakespeare, whose works are extensively read, is real-estate in London. Let Bill Smith, equally with Mr. Shakespeare now deceased, have as complete a control over his copyright as he would over his real-estate. Let him gamble it away, drink it away, or—give it to the church. Let his heirs and assigns treat it in the same manner.

"Every now and again I go up to Washington, sitting on a board to drive that sort of view into Congress. Congress takes its arguments against international copyright delivered ready made, and—Congress isn't very strong. I put the real-estate view of the case before one of the Senators.

"He said: 'Suppose a man has written a book that will live for ever?'

"I said: 'Neither you nor I will ever live to see that man, but we'll assume it. What then?'

"He said: 'I want to protect the world against that man's heirs and assigns, working under your theory.'

"I said: 'You think that all the world has no commercial sense. The book that will live for ever can't be artificially kept up at inflated prices. There will always be very expensive editions of it and cheap ones issuing side by side.'

"Take the case of Sir Walter Scott's novels," Mark Twain continued, turning to me. "When the copyright notes protected them, I bought editions as expensive as I could afford, because I liked them. At the same time the same firm were selling editions that a cat might buy. They had their real-estate, and not being fools, recognised that one portion of the plot could be worked as a gold mine, another as a vegetable garden, and another as a marble quarry. Do you see?"

What I saw with the greatest clearness was Mark Twain being forced to fight for the simple proposition that a man has as much right to the work of his brains (think of the heresy of it!) as to the labour of his hands. When the old lion roars, the young whelps growl. I growled assentingly, and the talk ran on from books in general to his own in particular.

Growing bold, and feeling that I had a few hundred thousand folk at my back, I demanded whether Tom Sawyer married Judge Thatcher's daughter and whether we were ever going to hear of Tom Sawyer as a man.

"I haven't decided," quoth Mark Twain, getting up, filling his pipe, and walking up and down the room in his slippers. "I have a notion of writing the sequel to 'Tom Sawyer' in two ways. In one I would make him rise to great honour and go to Congress, and in the other I should hang him. Then the friends and enemies of the book could take their choice."

Here I lost my reverence completely, and protested against any theory of the sort, because, to me at least, Tom Sawyer was real.

"Oh, he *is* real," said Mark Twain. "He's all the boy that I have known or recollect; but that would be a good way of ending the book"; then, turning round, "because, when you come to think of it, neither religion, training, nor education avails anything against the force of circumstances that drive a man. Suppose we took the next four-and-twenty years of Tom Sawyer's life, and gave a little joggle to the circumstances that controlled him. He would, logically and according to the joggle, turn out a rip or an angel."

"Do you believe that, then?"

"I think so. Isn't it what you call Kismet?"

"Yes: but don't give him two joggles and show the result, because he isn't your property any more. He belongs to us."

He laughed—a large, wholesome laugh—and this began a dissertation on the rights of a man to do what he liked with his own creations, which being a matter of purely professional interest, I will mercifully omit.

Returning to the big chair, he, speaking of truth and the like in literature, said that an autobiography was the one work in which a man, against his own will and in spite of his utmost striving to the contrary, revealed himself in his true light to the world.

"A good deal of your life on the Mississippi is autobiographical, isn't it?" I asked.

"As near as it can be—when a man is writing to a book and about himself. But in genuine autobiography, I believe it is impossible for a man to tell the truth about himself or to avoid impressing the reader with the truth about himself.

"I made an experiment once. I got a friend of mine—a man painfully given to speak the truth on all occasions—a man who wouldn't dream of telling a lie—and I made him write his autobiography for his own amusement and mine. He did it. The manuscript would have made an octavo volume, but—good, honest man that he was—in every single detail of his life that I knew about he turned out, on paper, a formidable liar. He could not help himself.

"It is not in human nature to write the truth about itself. None the less the reader gets a general impression from an autobiography whether the man is a fraud or a good man. The reader can't give his reasons any more than a man can explain why a woman struck him as being lovely when he doesn't remember her hair, eyes, teeth, or figure. And the impression that the reader gets is a correct one."

"Do you ever intend to write an autobiography?"

"If I do, it will be as other men have done—with the most earnest desire to make myself out to be the better man in every little business that has been to my discredit; and I shall fail, like the others, to make my readers believe anything except the truth."

This naturally led to a discussion on conscience. Then said Mark Twain, and his words are mighty and to be remembered:—

"Your conscience is a nuisance. A conscience is like a child. If you pet it and play with it and let it have everything that it wants, it becomes spoiled and intrudes on all your amusements and most of your griefs. Treat your conscience as you would treat anything else. When it is rebellious, spank it—be severe with it, argue with it, prevent it from coming to play with you at all hours, and you will secure a good conscience; that is to say, a properly trained one. A spoiled one simply destroys all the pleasure in life. I think I have reduced mine to order. At least, I haven't heard from it for some time. Perhaps I have killed it from over-severity. It's wrong to kill a child, but, in spite of all I have said, a conscience differs from a child in many ways. Perhaps it's best when it's dead."

Here he told me a little—such things as a man may tell a stranger—of his early life and upbringing, and in what manner he had been influenced for good by the example of his parents. He spoke always through his eyes, a light under the heavy eyebrows; anon crossing the room with a step as light as a girl's, to show me some book or other; then resuming his walk up and down the room, puffing at the cob-pipe. I would have given much for nerve enough to demand the gift of that pipe—value, five cents when new. I understood why certain savage tribes ardently desired the liver of brave men slain in combat. That pipe would have given me, perhaps, a hint of his keen insight into the souls of men. But he never laid it aside within stealing reach.

Once, indeed, he put his hand on my shoulder. It was an investiture of the Star of India, blue silk, trumpets, and diamond-studded jewel, all complete. If hereafter, in the changes and chances of this mortal life, I fall to cureless ruin, I will tell the superintendent of the workhouse that Mark Twain once put his hand on my shoulder; and he shall give me a room to myself and a double allowance of paupers' tobacco.

"I never read novels myself," said he, "except when the popular persecution forces me to—when people plague me to know what I think of the last book that every one is reading."

"And how did the latest persecution affect you?"

"Robert?" said, he, interrogatively.

I nodded.

"I read it, of course, for the workmanship. That made me think I had neglected novels too long—that there might be a good many books as graceful in style somewhere on the shelves; so I began a course of novel reading. I have dropped it now; it did not amuse me. But as regards Robert, the effect on me was exactly as though a singer of street ballads were to hear excellent music from a church organ. I didn't stop to ask whether the music was legitimate or necessary. I listened, and I liked what I heard. I am speaking of the grace and beauty of the style.

"You see," he went on, "every man has his private opinion about a book. But that is my private opinion. If I had lived in the beginning of things, I should have looked around the township to see what popular opinion thought of the murder of Abel before I openly condemned Cain. I should have had my private opinion, of course, but I shouldn't have expressed it until I had felt the way. You have my private opinion about that book. I don't know what my public ones are exactly. They won't upset the earth."

He curled himself into the chair and talked of other things.

"I spend nine months of the year at Hartford. I have long ago satisfied myself that there is no hope of doing much work during those nine months. People come in and call. They call at all hours, about everything in the world. One day I thought I would keep a list of interruptions. It began this way:—

"A man came and would see no one but Mr. Clemens. He was an agent for photogravure reproductions of Salon pictures. I very seldom use Salon pictures in my books.

"After that man another man, who refused to see any one but Mr. Clemens, came to make me write to Washington about something. I saw him. I saw a third man, then a fourth. By this time it was noon. I had grown tired of keeping the list. I wished to rest.

"But the fifth man was the only one of the crowd with a card of his own. He sent up his card. 'Ben Koontz, Hannibal, Mo.' I was raised in Hannibal. Ben was an old schoolmate of mine. Consequently I threw the house wide open and rushed with both hands out at a big, fat, heavy man, who was not the Ben I had ever known—nor anything like him.

"'But *is* it you, Ben?' I said. 'You've altered in the last thousand years.'

"The fat man said: 'Well, I'm not Koontz exactly, but I met him down in Missouri, and he told me to be sure and call on you, and he gave me his card, and'—here he acted the little scene for my benefit—'if you can wait a minute till I can get out the circulars—I'm not Koontz exactly, but I'm travelling with the fullest line of rods you ever saw.'"

"And what happened?" I asked breathlessly.

"I shut the door. He was not Ben Koontz—exactly—not my old school-fellow, but I had shaken him by both hands in love, and . . . I had been bearded by a lightning-rod man in my own house.

"As I was saying, I do very little work in Hartford. I come here for three months every year, and I work four or five hours a day in a study down the garden of that little house on the hill. Of course, I do not object to two or three interruptions. When a man is in the full swing of his work these little things do not affect him. Eight or ten or twenty interruptions retard composition."

I was burning to ask him all manner of impertinent questions, as to which of his works he himself preferred, and so forth; but, standing in awe of his eyes, I dared not. He spoke on, and I listened, grovelling.

It was a question of mental equipment that was on the carpet, and I am still wondering whether he meant what he said.

"Personally I never care for fiction or storybooks. What I like to read about are facts and statistics of any kind. If they are only facts about the raising of radishes, they interest me. Just now, for instance, before you came in"—he pointed to an encyclopaedia on the shelves—"I was reading an article about 'Mathematics.' Perfectly pure mathematics.

"My own knowledge of mathematics stops at 'twelve times twelve,' but I enjoyed that article immensely. I didn't understand a word of it; but facts, or what a man believes to be facts, are always delightful. That mathematical fellow believed in his facts. So do I. Get your facts first, and"—the voice dies away to an almost inaudible drone—"then you can distort 'em as much as you please."

Bearing this precious advice in my bosom, I left; the great man assuring me with gentle kindness that I had not interrupted him in the least. Once outside the door, I yearned to go back and ask some questions—it was easy enough to think of them now—but his time was his own, though his books belonged to me.

I should have ample time to look back to that meeting across the graves of the days. But it was sad to think of the things he had not spoken about.

In San Francisco the men of "The Call" told me many legends of Mark's apprenticeship in their paper five-and-twenty years ago; how he was a reporter delightfully incapable of reporting according to the needs of the day. He preferred, so they said, to coil himself into a heap and meditate until the last minute. Then he would produce copy bearing no sort of relationship to his legitimate work—copy that made the editor swear horribly, and the readers of "The Call" ask for more.

I should like to have heard Mark's version of that, with some stories of his joyous and variegated past. He has been journeyman printer (in those days he wandered from the banks of the Missouri even to Philadelphia), pilot-cub and full-blown pilot, soldier of the South (that was for three weeks only), private secretary to a Lieutenant-Governor of Nevada (that displeased him), miner, editor, special correspondent in the Sandwich Islands, and the Lord only knows what else. If so experienced a man could by any means be made drunk, it would be a glorious thing to fill him up with composite liquors, and, in the language of his own country, "let him retrospect." But these eyes will never see that orgy fit for the gods!

INDEX